GOD
—— IN THE ——
BALANCE

Other books by Carter Heyward from The Pilgrim Press

A Priest Forever (1976/2001)

Speaking of Christ: A Lesbian Feminist Voice,
edited by Ellen C. Davies (1989)

*Our Passion for Justice: Images of Power, Sexuality,
and Liberation* (1989)

When Boundaries Betray Us (1993/1999)

*Staying Power: Reflections on Gender, Justice,
and Compassion* (1995/2001)

GOD

—— IN THE ——
BALANCE

Christian Spirituality in Times of Terror

Carter Heyward

THE
PILGRIM
PRESS
Cleveland

In memory of

My beloved friend and soulmate
Angela (1926–2002), mystic, artist, prophet

My father, Bob (1915–1984),
a truly good man, veteran of World War II,
often remembered as "the good war"

Abdul Ghaffar Khan (d. 1988),
Afghani Pashtun pacifist,
sometimes called "the frontier Gandhi"

The Pilgrim Press, 700 Prospect Avenue, Cleveland, Ohio 44115-1100
pilgrimpress.com

Biblical quotations, unless otherwise noted, are from the New Revised Standard Version of the Bible, © 1989 by the Division of Christian Education of the National Council of Churches of Christ in the U.S.A., and are used by permission. Alterations have been made to make passages more inclusive.

07   06   05   04   03   02   5   4   3   2   1

Library of Congress Cataloging-in-Publication Data
Heyward, Carter.
   God in the balance : Christian spirituality in times of terror /
Carter Heyward.
     p. cm.
   Includes bibliographical references (p.).
   ISBN 0-8298-1517-1 (pbk. : alk. paper)
   1. Feminist theology. I. Title.

BT83.55 .H47 2002
261.8'73–dc21
                       2002025780

Proceeds from this book will go to Free Rein Center for Therapeutic Riding and Education in Brevard, N.C., and to Western Carolinians for Criminal Justice in Asheville, N.C., organizations committed to the social and ethical principles lifted up in these pages.

Contents

Acknowledgments   7

Prologue: Christmas Morning 2001   9

Introduction: God in the Balance   11

Part One
GOD OF WAR AND GOD OF PEACE

1. Warriors for Peace?   31

2. Too Late for Peace?   47

Part Two
GOD AS FATHER AND GOD AS SPIRIT

3. Transforming the Father   53

4. Beyond Shameful Theology   67

Part Three
GOD IN US AND GOD IN ALL

5. Creatures in the Image of (a Morally Complex) God   73

6. The Horse as Priest   92

Epilogue: An Almost Unbearable Lightness of Being
In Celebration of Sister Angela   97

Notes   105

Selected Readings   109

Acknowledgments

Thanks to the people at home — Sue Sasser, Bev Harrison, and Debra Sue Chenault — and the folks at the Stables at Las Praderas, especially Carolyn Bane, Liz Galloway, and Hollan Schwartz, for helping make time and space in our life together in the fall of 2001 for me to undertake this project; to Sue Hiatt, who struggles bravely to sit, stand, walk, and to Linda Levy, equestrian extraordinaire, for helping radicalize my understanding of "balance"; to Michael West of Fortress Press and Timothy Staveteig of The Pilgrim Press, for their brotherly solidarity and good editorial sense in helping shepherd this manuscript toward publication; and to all the creatures that "go with," especially "Mr. Brennan," special needs miracle dog companion, "Sugar," the horse who smiles, and the pair of pileated woodpeckers who worked on the suet as I typed.

Christmas Morning 2001

O little town of Kabul,
how still we see thee lie.
Above thy stones and weary bones
the silent stars go by.
Few ears can hear thy crying
amid the rubble and the dust.
Still God imparts to human hearts
a wisdom and a trust.

For you it is your imam,
your ikhlas and jihad.
For Jews it is the Torah
and the one most holy G-d.
For others many sacred ones
who come by many names,
Brigitte, Kwan Yin, Krishna,
countless others, none the same.

Yet God imparts to human hearts
a truth that sets us free.
Among the many, there is one,
a way of peace,
and here's the key.
While none can fully live it
and none can rightly claim
to own the holy name,
all can taste its sweetness,
all can know its kiss,
all are promised this.

It's a way we're meant to share,
a way to love, a way to care
about Afghanis and Israelis
Palestinians and Kurds,
about brothers round the earth,
and women's sacred worth,
about strangers and our kin,
whether enemy or friend,
about animals and land,
about water, trees, and wind.

Their spirits gather with us
round the baby born today,
round the baby born in dust and hay,
who came in the morning
to spark our deep yearning
to be love-bearers filled
with compassion and zest,
who came to befriend us,
to live here among us,
to celebrate with us
ourselves at our best.

This we see again today
through babies being born
in the squalor and the hay
in little towns like Bethlehem.
How still we see them lie
above the stones and weary bones
as silent stars go by.

Few eyes will see her coming
amid the rubble and the din,
but come to us, abide with us,
sweet Jesus, be our friend.

God in the Balance

God hold you in this turning,
Christ warm you through this night,
Spirit breathe its ancient rhythm,
Peace give your sorrows flight.[1]
— Jan L. Richardson

How might those of us who are Christians in the United States today respond to the violence and terror that struck such a mighty blow against this nation in September 2001? How might we also respond to the "war against terrorism" being waged in retaliation? Is there anything we can learn from our own faith tradition — about terrorism and the war against it — that might empower us to become a more active, radically prayerful, creative, and liberating movement for justice and compassion, peace and social transformation? These deep, persistent questions were posed for me by the events of September 11, 2001. I've been wanting to write a small "faith manifesto" for a long time. But I've actually needed to do it in the aftermath of the terrorist events and the subsequent violence being waged by the United States.

This book is about God, which is not an unusual topic for a theologian. It's about our life *in God* — a little more unusual for a Christian theologian, since Christians tend to portray God as a "someone," a "person" in whose image we are made and who relates to us as "more" than a spiritual energy in which we live. Those familiar with my work probably will not be surprised by anything in these pages, except maybe my interest in God as "Father" and God as "Warrior," theological images both prim-

11

itive and contemporary. But the primary message I am hoping to convey through these pages is that we find and are found by God, our sacred power for radical mutuality, in the midst of life, including war and patriarchy. Faithful religious experience, more than anything, is a matter of being able to keep our balance in the midst of competitive, often oppositional, currents.

In this small volume of essays, I am suggesting a path for a Christian spirituality that may help us in a world in which absolutist doctrines and ideologies — including fierce nationalisms and culturisms — are at war for our bodies and minds. It is important for us to learn spiritually how to bend and sway, how not to go rigid, in the face of terror. The last thing the world needs is more self-righteousness among people who know that their way, or our way, is not only best but is God's way and the only way for humankind. There may be a degree of separation between the terrorist theology that fueled the planes on September 11 and the Christian theology that undergirds military efforts to wipe out our enemies, but I am not sure there is much difference at all.

Like you, I was stunned and appalled by the events of September 11. I have been struggling with anger, grief, and fear, knocked off balance by the attacks. Although I lost no personal friends or colleagues on that horrific day, I feel as if I did because, as many others have acknowledged, we all lost a great deal on that day in the early fall of 2001.

This book is meant to illustrate what seems to me at stake when Christians gather to worship and try to make sense of our lives spiritually, morally, and politically, especially now in these times that are being shaped by the "war against terrorism." Of course, it's too soon for us to conclude much of anything about the "larger" meanings of what happened on September 11 and what is happening now. But it's not too soon for us to be thinking together about our lives, including matters of faith — what we believe, what we value, how we act, how we worship — and how our Christian faith, even now, may need re-forming under the threat of terrorism and the war against it.

I offer these reflections as a resource for what I have long believed to be a much needed reformation in Christian doctrine and worship, especially in the part of Christendom I know best: mainstream, predominantly white, Protestantism, including the Episcopal/Anglican tradition, in the United States. Terrorism and the struggle against it has sharpened my theological sensibilities and has made such a Christian reformation seem all the more urgent.

I am sure that one significant key to our salvation as a planet and certainly as a human species is in how we experience and image God. We live our lives, and wage our wars or our peace, on the basis of how we perceive ourselves in relation to God. What we believe matters. How we worship matters. What we name God matters more than most Christian liberals and radicals have realized, because our language codifies and carries our ethics and priorities across religions, cultures, generations, and international boundaries.

It is time for us to stop shaping our worship and our lives around violent and oppressive God-images. It is time for us to become agents of theological and social transformation, and that is what this book is about.

The three pairs of images explored here — God of War and God of Peace, God as Father and God as Spirit, God in Us and God in All — are rooted in long-standing theological issues, theoethical tensions, and social and pastoral questions. Moreover, each of these tensions represents a massive arena of global turmoil in this new, twenty-first, century.

The struggle between a God of War and a God of Peace is steeped in our experiences of terrorism and violence and war. The pull between God as Father and God as Spirit is the classical struggle between patriarchal religion and the opening of human experience to women's sacred power and to the fundamental sacredness of all creation. The tension between our experiences of God in Us and God in All others reflects not only the temptation to assume that our own culture and religion is best and truest but also that our human species is more important

_____ **Figure 1:**

Images of God	Foundational Theological Issues
God of War / God of Peace	Good and evil Nature of God
God as Father / God as Spirit	Sacred (creative, liberating) power
God in Us / God in All	Creation Nature of humankind

to God than the lives of other creatures. These self-centered assumptions are the breeding ground not only for racism and other forms of social injustice but also for the domination and destruction of the earth and its many varied creatures.

This book calls us to live together in the balance between and among these experiences and images of God. It also calls us to realize that each experience and image of God is touched and transformed by other experiences and images. God not only is the power of mutuality that sparks such transformation. God is also a Sacred Power that is eternally being moved and changed, formed and re-formed, in our life together on earth. This means, for example, that the Father-God can become for us the Mother-God or the Warrior-God or the Truth-Force or many other experiences and images of Sacred Power — depending upon context and need. In this book, we will look at several images of God that have been important to Christians. There are so many others that we could be exploring here, and that need attention. I hope that, together, we can turn our attention to some of the others in times to come.

The Challenge of Terrorism

What happened on September 11 was the result of many things, including demented theological thinking. So massive was the damage that we cannot know all that has been lost,

The Tensions of God in the Balance _____

Theoethical Tensions	Social, Moral-Ethical, and Pastoral Questions
Just war / Nonviolent resistance	How can we move beyond violence and terror?
Sacred power as domination / Sacred power as mutuality	How can we transform patriarchy?
Us-centered / All-centered Human-centered / Creation-centered	How can we create alternatives to the destruction of "alien" humans, creatures, and earth?

but surely we see that much of what is best among us was badly shaken — our ability to trust, our desire to welcome the stranger, our belief in the basic goodness of our sister and brother humans including those whom we do not know, and our deepest yearnings for peace on earth, goodwill to all.

Regardless of who wages it or for what purpose, terrorism is evil because it attacks our human capacity to love one another, including our enemies. It is a violent social movement, often motivated by worthy political goals and undertaken against individuals against whom its perpetrators hold no personal grievance. In that sense, terrorism is an impersonal violent campaign waged against anyone who happens to belong to a particular religious, national, ethnic, racial, gender, or sexual group or tribe or, in many cases, such as on September 11, 2001, anyone who happens to be in the wrong place at the wrong time.

The primary motive of terrorism is not to kill or destroy, but to terrorize a population — to show people that the targets of violence could be anyone, even us, next time; and that there's nothing we can do about it, except brace ourselves and tighten up everything from our national security to our minds. Terrorists mean to make us all feel vulnerable, even paranoid, wondering what might happen next and who the perpetrators might be: The nice quiet guy who lives down the hall and keeps to himself — I think he's received some mysterious packages.

That passenger in the first row — doesn't she look odd to you? The boy standing on the corner — what's he doing there at this time of night? The Middle Eastern looking man entering the theater — who's he with?

What happened in New York, Washington, and the field in Pennsylvania was "terrorist" in its effects because it left people in the United States profoundly frightened and edging toward paranoia. A number of public commentators noted during the following weeks and months that people in the United States seemed to be suffering from "PTSD" — post-traumatic stress disorder — a term psychologists heretofore have used mainly to describe *individuals'* experiences of instability and agitation that often follow their having been violently assaulted. "September 11" left the United States of America[2] reeling collectively, not just as individuals. Consequently, in our terror, we are in danger of becoming a paranoid nation — one that sees an enemy behind every dark face and a terrorism-supporter behind every speech or demonstration that is critical of the United States foreign or domestic policies.

Context of Terrorism

It might help us keep ourselves — this nation, the rest of the world, and the evil of terrorism — in perspective if we realize that what happened to the United States in September 2001, outrageous as it was, was one of many terrorist acts that have been waged historically against our brothers and sisters. Our life together as a global people, and as a nation, is littered with terror. Some of it we have bravely fought — Hitler and the Nazis provide one of the clearest instances of the United States struggling against state-sponsored terrorism. More recently, women and their allies in the United States and elsewhere have boldly resisted the terrorism of some of the more violent, even murderous, anti-abortion activists. But in our national conversations about terrorism, we need to be aware that much terrorism has also come in the form of our own agenda as a nation, our own foreign and domestic policies, which most of us in the United States have never understood as "terrorism." We insist, for example, that we did not intend to bring harm to people on the Middle Passage, along the Trail of Tears, in Hiroshima, Japan, or My Lai, Vietnam; just as we did not intend the slaughter of college students, journalists, and housewives in Chile when we helped orchestrate the murder of Salvador Allende and many thousands in the wake of this brutal U.S.-sponsored coup in 1973. And of course our leaders insist that we do not intend today to be terrorizing the citizens of the world who are mistakenly hit by our cluster bombs.

The United States — I speak here of our federal government, which we allow to speak for us — too often shapes the morality of its policies and actions around good intentions rather than actual impact. Since, like most nations, we intend to do good, we are inclined to blame others for their own troubles and often for ours as well. We are able to use our struggle with others — an enemy like "terrorism" — as an excuse not only for making war but also for the practice of injustice here at home. As I write, the U.S. is laying blame for most of its troubles, domestically as well as globally, on Osama bin Laden, Al Qaeda, and the Taliban. By the time this book is published, in the summer of 2002, no telling who we will be naming as the enemy. Ten years ago it was Saddam Hussein. As recently as two decades ago, it was the Russians and Communism that were responsible for just about every evil under the sun. During World War II, it was the Japanese whom we seemed most to fear and hate; and while no doubt there are military reasons that can be used to explain why we dropped The Bomb on cities in Japan, not Germany, must we not wonder what role racism played in this strategic selection?

As for racism, it has never been clear to me whom we blame for the twin terrors of slavery and the near extinction of indigenous North Americans. The closest thing to a theological justification I heard as a child was that "white people" (European Christians) were trying to "save savages" in both cases, but first we white folks had to decide if these savages had "souls." As of today, the United States has made no serious attempt to apologize for these morally horrific instances of state-sponsored terrorism, much less to make amends to African Americans and Native Americans. What are we as a nation afraid of should we seek to make amends for the evils that we have done? Litigation is the current excuse. We are afraid that any official attempt to make amends for the wrongs that we have inflicted on one another here at home would precipitate litigation against the federal government and might strip resources from our military budget or land from our people. But could it be also that we are afraid that we as a nation might appear to ourselves and others to be weak and vulnerable? I believe that *the appearance of moral weakness* troubles us most, more even than the possible loss of money or land, which likely would be resolved in any case through the processes of making restitution, though not without protracted struggle.

The United States of America cannot bear to be seen as a nation that, over the course of time, has made mistakes that have resulted in massive suffering. We worry that such an admission would constitute a moral erasure of all the good that we also have done at home and abroad, in times past and present. A proud nation, we have no intention of being shamed and embarrassed, and we are not well developed, as a people, in living in tension and ambiguity, not skillful at standing in the balance among competing perceptions of who we are or who other nations and peoples are. It's hard for U.S. citizens to see the United States and other nations too as having both excellent and terrible features. Our inability to live gracefully in this important moral tension is a spiritual problem.

But there is more. Over the last half-century and now into the twenty-first, the United States has been concerned that admitting our mistakes, at home and abroad, and beginning to make amends might open us to more than serious moral and legal wrestling among ourselves. We have been worried that such confessions would make us seem materially (militarily and economically) weak, thus more physically vulnerable to our enemies, more likely targets of attack should those who hate us wish to harm us.

Vulnerability: Openness to Mutuality

All of this shifted on September 11, 2001, as we were left stunned in the realization of how vulnerable we are, even in the midst of our wealth, our pride, and our power as a nation. We were attacked by those who presumably do hate us. And while nothing can justify what happened that day, the better part of wisdom is for us to try to understand the social, political, and theological frameworks within which this particular terrorist and, now, anti-terrorist war is being waged.[3] Since that September morning, most people in the United States have felt more vulnerable. Most of us have felt pretty wiped out in the months following the attacks, but our vulnerability need not continue to pull us down. For despite the despicable occasion that triggered it, vulnerability need not be a debilitating psychospiritual or social condition. For at its root, vulnerability is about openness, not weakness — openness to our need for one another, openness to mutuality.

Vulnerability is a context in which theology ought to be done, because vulnerability and mutuality are rich spiritual soil. So, while many others are addressing the political, historical, social, economic, and cultural implications of the attack on the United States, this small book explores, from a specifically Christian perspective, some of the theological implications of terrorism in the twenty-first century — and the struggle against it, especially for those of us who are Christians in the United States.

Elsewhere I've discussed fear as the chief demon among all the various psychospiritual forces that compete for allegiance in our daily lives. In this book, I use the term "terror" as a synonym for intense, unabating fear. I'm writing to Christians who are terrorized in these times or who are working with those who are. Terror can either push us into senses of powerlessness and despair or it can become a springboard into wellsprings of vulnerability in which we help one another learn more fully what it is to be human — mutual and interdependent — in times like these, times of terror, grief, and anger.

Grief is a psychological, social, and spiritual resource we share today, in response to terrorism and the war against it. We ought not deny or underestimate the toll that grief is taking on us as a people, regardless of what losses each of us personally may have incurred through these events. Grief is an embodied response not only to personal loss, such as the death of a spouse, a lover, a child, or a friend; it is also a response to the shattering of illusions and to the realization that a significant change has taken place in our life together.

Why are so many of us making pilgrimages to "ground zero" and to the altars of pictures, flowers, poems, and candles that have sprung up around New York, Washington, and in the Pennsylvania field? Why, on the other hand, are so many of us refusing to go back to the site of the former World Trade Center or even to glance over toward the hole in the sky in lower Manhattan as we travel along the New Jersey Turnpike? Grief is a powerful force; like fear and anger, it can be a resource for important spiritual breakthroughs and theological insights.

A third psychospiritual and social response to the terrorist attacks and, for many of us, to the Bush administration's war on terrorism as well, has been anger. In an essay translated into many languages and read throughout the world as a classic in feminist social ethics, Beverly Harrison writes about "the power of anger in the work of love."[4] Her essay has evoked strong appreciation because in it, Harrison, a Christian ethicist, recognizes the positive, creative character of anger in helping us live justice-seeking, compassionate lives. She contends that, if we are paying attention to our own bodies, we can experience our anger as a signal that there is a problem that often can be addressed. Our anger becomes a creative energy for change. Is this not where the terrorist attacks and the war on terrorism put many of us today — in anger as well as fear and grief, wondering what if anything we ourselves can do? Can we learn from our anger how to live together in peace with justice?

This book reflects what my anger, along with my grief and fear, has been teaching me about God — specifically, about our need as Christians to open up to greater diversity of peoples and cultures and even species as God-bearers. One of the church's basic spiritual problems, a problem that has plagued Christianity and other patriarchal religious traditions from the beginning, has been the making of God in the image of those men who rule the world. It is easy enough for people in the United States to condemn the Taliban for the spectacular misogyny of their religious practice. How much harder it is for Christians to be honest and clear about the patriarchal character of our own faith tradition, and ways in which Christian sexism and heterosexism continue to shape life in the United States and around the world.

Our Images of God: Why They Matter

In this book I take a look at six different images of God. Each is important to some — in several cases, many — Christians in the United States and elsewhere today: God of War, or Warrior God, and God of Peace, which I am suggesting is the same spirit as *satyagraha* (Gandhi's term for truth-force or soul-force); God as Father and God as Spirit; and God in Us, the image of God in humans, especially humans "like us," and God in All, the image of God in other creatures and in humans whom we experience as "alien." We could be exploring many pairs of God-images here: Intimate Friend and Absent (No) God, Liberator God and God of Reason, Lord and Servant, Word (Logos) and Wisdom (Sophia) are images that sprang to mind immediately when I began thinking about this piece. Each of these images and many others have helped large numbers of Christians deal creatively — and often not so creatively — with fear, grief, and anger as well as with joy, gratitude, and courage. We live in the midst of these and many other experiences and images of sacred power. When we are living our most fully human lives, helping embody a fully divine Spirit among us, we are living beautifully, if often raggedly, in the balance of religious experiences that are tugging us in different directions. In the balance, we are better able to live each day in suppleness and confidence, better able to bend and turn and turn again to stay sane and creative in a world being shaped by terror.

I am not attempting in these pages to explore the specific events surrounding September 11, 2001, or the many spiritual and theological meanings that have been attached to it already by Christians, Muslims, Jews, and others. Like those responsible for most terrorist assaults throughout human history, those who schemed the attack on the United States no doubt try to justify it by their custom-made readings of their holy scriptures. Many, myself included, would say that such self-justifying "readings" of scripture to justify suffering, in defense of whatever terrorist act and in the name of whatever god, are spiritually twisted and morally bankrupt. Terrorism of any kind is profoundly unfaithful to any god of love, justice, and compassion.

So how do we Christians live faithfully and courageously in the context of a social order in which terrorism — a state of radical unfaithfulness — is threatening to shape our daily lives, much as it has always played a major role in the lives and destinies of people around the world? In this challenging social and political situation, does it matter who or what we worship? Does it matter how we experience and image God? Does it really matter what words and pictures we draw in our rituals, both more formally on Sunday mornings and less formally through cultural media such as movies, television, literature, commercials, billboards, marquees, and language? As Christians, how do our experiences and understandings of

God play into our responses not only to September 11 but to the larger challenges of living justice-seeking, compassionate, good-humored lives in the context of an increasingly terror-driven world? Perhaps most urgently, how does Christian theology provide some spiritual underpinnings for terrorism itself? And how might Christian theology help undermine this evil force and even play a role in the transformation of some terrorist energy into creative, rather than destructive, movements for justice in the world?

Several colleagues have asked if I plan to consider other religions in this little book, especially Islam and Judaism since, with Christianity, these ancient monotheistic traditions share a number of problems, beginning with the patriarchalism by which they secure the rights and privileges of men and boys.[5] I do indeed emphasize here the problem of patriarchy, which Christianity shares with Islam and Judaism. There's no way to write an honest piece on Christian theology without paying attention to the *problem* of the centrality of the "Father and Son." But I will not attempt here to explore Islam's or Judaism's sexism, heterosexism, or misogyny, partly because I do not have time to do the research that intelligent treatment would require but more importantly because it belongs to Muslim and Jewish feminists to challenge their own traditions.

Over the next few years, I imagine that much research will be undertaken by women and men of diverse religious traditions in an effort to provide different theological understandings of terrorism and the war against it, including the twin terrors of sexism and heterosexism that remain fashionable and death-dealing throughout much of the world and in all patriarchal religions. This book is about Christian theology, especially as practiced in the United States today.

Thinking Theologically, Living Faithfully

This book is for Christians and others interested in thinking about how theology in general, Christian theology in particular, affects how we live and act as nations, communities, and individuals, in the period of history following September 11, 2001. Christian "theology," for our purposes here, is what and how Christians *think about* God, Jesus Christ, Spirit, church, and related matters. Thinking well involves feeling deeply and being able to reflect on what our feelings are trying to tell us. Good theology requires strong feelings and clear thinking. Christian "spirituality" is how we actually *experience* God, Jesus, and Spirit.

Consider this analogy. A person is lying in bed, unable to sleep. If "spirituality" is like being unable to sleep, then "theology" is like thinking about how your body feels, how you feel emotionally, what happened earlier in the day that might have upset you, whether the mattress is comfortable, whether the room is too hot, whether there's too much noise outside, etc. If upon reflection you realize that the problem was the coffee you drank after supper, you might decide to forgo the caffeine next time. "Spirituality" is the raw material of spiritual experiences and "theology" is the process of thinking about these experiences to provide intelligent frameworks for future guidance.

Theology — how and what we think about God — certainly affects how we shape our lives, collectively and individually; and how we live also affects what we think about God. Thus, theology is a spiraling process, never ending. For this reason, you and I can be theologians involved in the shaping of Christian doctrine, worship, and life. We work in the legacies of those who've gone before us, in the company of those who go with us now, and in the spirit of those who will come after us. You and I are not here on planet earth simply to receive what has been passed on, theologically or otherwise. We are here to help make all things new — in the words of the Jewish writer Elie Wiesel, to "recreate the universe." What we do and how we think about what we do matters a great deal to God and to the universe, as well as to our sister and brother humans and other creatures.

The Three Theoethical Tensions

In this book I will not only be lifting up the six images of God as Warrior, God as Peace/Truth-Force, God as Father, God as Spirit, God in human being, and God in other-creature being. I present each of these images in relation to, and in tension with, another because that is how we experience them. The three theological tensions explored here — between God of war and God of peace, between Father and Spirit, between human and other creatures in the image of God — reflect the spiritual experiences of many Christians, especially liberal Protestants and Roman Catholics in the United States today. When our lives are spiritually "out of balance," these tensions keep us on edge, agitated, and afraid. This is the problem with the churches' resistance to opening up images of God and to moving beyond patriarchal renderings of God as Father, Son, Warrior, King, Lord, etc. It is also why many Christian women and some men no longer find this unbalanced spirituality helpful, healthy, or even possible in the most honest moments of our private and common prayer. It is not that there is no good place for our Father God, but his place cannot be the only one at the head of the table of Christian worship and hospitality.

These theological tensions are not new, nor are they all necessarily or exclusively Christian in character. In each case the pull is between images of God that Christians often think of (theologically) as opposite, and even conflictual, yet that we often experience (spiritually) as mutually related and interdependent. I am choosing to explore these particular six God-images because the social contexts in which we experience them are such strong, significant currents in our life together today: terrorism and the war against it; patriarchy; and environmental domination and destruction.

From a more encouraging perspective, I see God in many places and movements today, including these three overlapping contexts: (1) global efforts toward peace-building and nonviolent resistance; (2) the struggle for the liberation of all women, gays, lesbians, bisexual, transgender, and other queer people; and (3) our learning together how to care for the earth and its many varied creatures. In these times of terror and anti-terror, we must think about how our understandings of God play into the dynamics of war-making and peace-building. Because we in the United States, like most of humankind and creaturekind, are still living under patriarchal rules and customs, the Christian pull between Father and Spirit continues to be enormously important in our shared life. Finally, the relation between, on the one hand, humanity's understanding of itself as the image of God and, on the other, our recognition of God in our sister and brother creatures, reflects a significant strain in our life together. If I had time at this point, I would have added a fourth theological tension that is at least as powerful as the others — that between images of Lord and Servant, which could be examined in the context of global capitalism. This is certainly a tension with which the church should be wrestling theologically, liturgically, ethically, and pastorally.

God as Mother

In the midst of it all, where does God as Mother fit into this scheme of primary Christian imaging? Thinking about the places among us of a God who is Mother — lifting her up in our worship, worshiping her with our lives — poses a formidable challenge to Christians as it does to all patriarchal religion. Roman Catholics historically have turned to Mary as a means of incorporating a mother-image of God. Despite (or perhaps because of) her immense appeal as an icon of divine power among masses of faithful Catholics throughout the world, Mary has been given no official recognition alongside her son Jesus as God. Such recognition would constitute a radical shift in how the church actually understands and worships God as Father, Son, and Spirit.

To recognize Mary as God would redefine the Trinity in such a way as to make space for God the Mother. To open up the Trinity in this way would be profoundly faithful to the deepest meanings of the doctrine of the Trinity, which are relational, dynamic, and inclusive. But the Magisterium of Roman Catholicism has shown repeatedly that it cares less about good theology than about holding patriarchal power in place, and Protestants have fared no better theologically. We have enjoyed no significant, much less sacred, images of Mary or other women in our worship or our communities. On the whole, we Protestants have produced liturgies and theologies remarkably devoid of sacred female energy, so devoid that we might conclude fairly that the shapers of Protestantism, like their Roman brothers, have been averse to strong female leadership and to images of holy women as powerful, beautiful, and large in size and significance.

Christians need to be warned, however, against superficially placing God the Mother alongside unrevised, patriarchal images of God the Father. Simply tagging on new images, without struggling to transform old ones, is a process that lacks theological integrity. This often happens among progressive Christians who are trying to be "inclusive" in language yet who resist movement toward significant theological change and spiritual transformation, perhaps because they do not want to but just as often because they do not know how to.

I am suggesting here that God the Father can become God the Mother; that the Divine Mother and Father can, together and separately, become many other experiences and images of God; and that these spiritual transformations take place through the power of the Spirit. Indeed, with or without the Father, our Mother God lives among us, depending upon context, as a friend, a sister, a colleague, a worker, an athlete, a lover, a warrior, a peacemaker, a companion to her child, whom we Christians usually call "Jesus" or "Christ" but whom we may also experience and name in countless ways, e.g., as any mother's child, homeless boy, spiritually attentive girl, brother or sister, neighbor or friend, stranger toward whom we can exercise hospitality, or enemy toward whom we can show mercy.

Organization of This Book

The book is divided into three parts following this introductory piece and the poem that precedes it. These parts focus on dynamics between God of War and God of Peace, God as Father and God as Spirit, and God in Us and God in All. Each part concludes with an essay written in the fall of 2001 for publication by daily newspapers or, in one case, a progressive religious journal.

Here as elsewhere, I am attempting to build on the best of "the old" in Christianity, theological traditions that many Christians continue to experience in tension with our life together in today's world.[6] A livable, liberating theology always requires a radical reimaging of the old in relation to a creative, courageous imaging of the new. Antiquity is constantly in the background and often a significant dimension of who we are in the present world. The past needs to be learned from and transformed into resources for a living faith. This is the theological task as well as the better part of wisdom today, as ever, for people of all cultures, nations, and religions.

Part One

God of War
and
God of Peace

⟡⟡⟡⟡⟡⟡⟡⟡

He shall judge between the nations,
and shall arbitrate for many peoples;
they shall beat their swords into plowshares,
and their spears into pruning hooks;
nation shall not lift up sword against nation,
neither shall they learn war any more.

—Isaiah 2:4

Blessed are the peacemakers
for they will be called children of God.

—Matthew 5:9

Warriors for Peace?

The United States' war against terrorism, at least in its early days, is as popular as World War II, which is sometimes referred to as "the good war." But can any war be "good"? If so, isn't even a "good war" an occasion for much evil? Most people in the U.S. and elsewhere in the world are clear that using commercial jetliners as bombs to destroy buildings filled with civilians is an evil act, anything but good. Yet there is little doubt that the young men who hijacked the planes on September 11, 2001, believed that they were sacrificing themselves for a higher good — waging war against an "infidel" power, the United States of America. Is this not the same sentiment that infuses all "good wars" from the perspectives of those who wage them?

What troubles many of us in this country and around the world is that, once again, the mightiest nation on earth has chosen simply to turn the tables and return in kind what has been given — violence for violence. Of course, we have many ways of justifying the bombs being rained down upon Afghanistan: We didn't start this war; "they" did. This nation and the world remain at peril as long as the Al Qaeda terrorist network is at large. And, unlike our adversaries, we do not intend to harm innocent people. If ever there was truly a "good war," we seem to have found it.

Moreover, as we see, this war we are making already seems to be liberating in important ways. It has been powerfully moving to see women removing their burqas, smiling, and heading off to school. Why, many have asked, did the United States not move more quickly against the Taliban? Was the brutalizing of women and girls not reason enough for us to make war against the evil oppressors?

The problem with this "good war" rhetoric and belief is that real life doesn't work this way. Writing in the fifth century C.E., the theologian Augustine suggested that a "just," "holy," or "good" war is sometimes necessary. Even so, Augustine taught, Christians must love their enemies and should never fight or kill anyone until they first love them. But how real is this? What does it mean to love our enemies? What does it mean to love before we fight and before we kill? Do you imagine that our soldiers are being spiritually disciplined to love the terrorists? Are we the people being challenged by George Bush to love Osama bin Laden? If the president-select of the United States were speaking to us of enemy-love at this point, we would be living in a spiritually transformed and transforming nation that had truly begun to win the war against terrorism. As it is, we will not win any war against terrorism; we will, like the terrorists against whom we struggle, simply fight and fight until our enemy is either dead or has surrendered.

So let's talk about love, not sweet dreams or idealistic notions, but the kind of love that *does* beat swords into plowshares. Let us imagine for a moment that this depth and quality of love is God — and that we can learn much about this God, this Love, by living honestly in the tension between a God of Peace and a Warrior God, One who can become for many a God of Terror. Perhaps we can imagine that, in the balance, a "good war" is possible and that soldiers can be warriors for peace.

Spirit of Peace: Nonviolent Truth-Force

Mohandas K. Gandhi is one of the most significant moral and spiritual leaders in the history of the world. Like his disciples, including Martin Luther King Jr. of the United States and Mary Robinson of Ireland, Gandhi has much to teach us, deep wisdom to offer in these times of terror. What makes Gandhi so compelling is that he was simply a person, very much one of us, like all great spiritual leaders, including Jesus. He was an average sort of man who was transformed by his experiences of violent struggle together with his reflections on the Bhagavat-Gita (Hindu sacred text) and the Sermon on the Mount from Christian scripture.

He was not a pacifist. Having witnessed the brutality of the violent struggle against racism in South Africa, where he worked as a young lawyer from 1893 to 1914, Gandhi began to develop strategies of nonviolent resistance to oppression as a means of confronting evil. Over time, and especially in India, where he led the successful campaign of nonviolent resistance to British rule, Gandhi's strategies became increasingly shaped by his thoroughgoing commitment to *ahimsa,* or nonviolence, as a way of life grounded in love. It was a spiritual commitment that Gandhi realized neither he nor anyone could live completely and without failure.

We might think of Gandhi as a warrior for peace. Like Arjuna, the warrior prince in the Gita, he was a social reformer who, early in his adult life, began to realize the awful truth about violence.[7] He saw that violence breeds violence, only more violence, not peace and not justice in any lasting way. It was as a young lawyer in South Africa that Gandhi witnessed the escalating character of violence and began to seek other, more effective, ways of bringing about social change. As Arjuna had turned to Sri Krishna, the Lord of Love, the young Gandhi also turned to this spiritual power in order to learn how to break what Dom Helder Camara, the great Brazilian bishop of Recife, would later name "the spiral of violence." Gandhi recognized Sri Krishna, the great Spirit of Love, in the life of Jesus and other great lovers of God and the world. Like Jesus, Gandhi began to realize that love is the only force that can break the spiral of violence. He recognized that Hinduism and Christianity, like all rich moral traditions, teach that God is above all the Spirit of Love. Of Christianity, Gandhi is said to have remarked, "It's a beautiful religion which is seldom practiced" — a sentiment, I might add, shared by many Christians.

For Gandhi, a good warrior against evil was, more than anything, a man or woman rooted and grounded in what Gandhi named *satyagraha,* a Gujarati term that in English means "soulforce" or "truth-force." From a Christian perspective, we might say that *satyagraha* is the Holy Spirit, in which Jesus lived and in which the rest of us also are called to live and breathe and have our being. In the Holy Spirit, or *satyagraha,* a good, just, or holy war would be a movement against an enemy that is steeped in a commitment to love our enemy.

Concretely, such enemy-love would involve, at the very least, a recognition of the basic human rights of those against whom we fight. We would not be trumpeting a triumphalist determination to wipe out our enemy. We would rather be seeking ways that would necessarily involve other nations and peoples throughout the world, seeking ways to subdue the enemy — literally to disarm the enemy — and to treat the enemy with the guarantee of fairness that love requires.

Without enemy-love, any violence that we wage — even against those who would destroy us — is not holy. It is not just. It is not good. It is simply an effort to protect ourselves or to exact retribution and vengeance. The "military tribunals" that Bush, Ashcroft, and other U.S. leaders are calling for represent nothing good or just, because they are steeped not in enemy-love but in anger, fear, and hatred of our enemies. For this reason, they are an offense to the Christian God of Love, the Spirit of a Good Warrior. We delude ourselves if we imagine that this God, the One whom Jesus loved, is somehow on our side when we ourselves are not loving our enemies.

The United States has much to learn from those nations like Spain that have indicated that they will not extradite to the U.S. people who are accused of terrorism because they do not believe such prisoners can receive fair treatment either through military tribunals or from a justice system in which people can be executed. Spain is right about this. The United States is wrong. It is vital that Christians and other religious people in the U.S. speak up about ways in which our own nation is fostering injustice at home and abroad and, in so doing, is generating dynamics that will result in more terrorism.

But what then, many wonder, can be done with terrorist leaders when they are captured? What do we do with these people if we do not kill them? I am sure there are no simple answers. And I am also sure that here, as in so many situations, the United States needs to be working with, not against, other nations to answer this question and others like it. We need not go it alone nor insist upon being first or best in peace-building. We need to participate in, rather than resist the leadership of, the United Nations. We need to join with other nations in forging an international coalition to generate multilateral responses to terrorism as well as to other evils that threaten not just the United States but the whole world.

For followers of Jesus, God can be imaged as a warrior, but only as a good warrior — one struggling alongside others for peace. This God is always *satyagraha* — truth-force, soul-force, connecting us with others in the ongoing struggles for justice and peace. God is never a spirit of vengeance or rage to be hurled at others, as if "we" embody all goodness and "they," all evil.

It is possible — and morally imperative and strategically wise — for the U.S. to condemn terrorism without demonizing every nation and person who questions how the United States is going about waging the "war on terrorism." It is also important that U.S. citizens realize that true patriotism, love of country, is broad and deep enough to welcome questions about how our nation is building war and even whether or not we should be waging this war.

As it is, for now, those U.S. citizens who protest the way the war against terrorism is being constructed in this nation and elsewhere will be viewed by many of our compatriots as "unpatriotic." We might find it helpful to recall that this is what happened in the 1950s to people who raised questions about the demonization of all communist sympathies and socialist commitments. In retrospect, McCarthyism has been recognized as a wildly excessive and abusive response to communism. Are we now at the dawn of a new McCarthyism — this time, a Bushism — in which the new enemy is terrorism instead of communism and in which repression at home and imperialism abroad will be justified as necessary to national security?

Who Is the "Good Warrior"?

Our churches today could be teaching us something important about God and Christian life if, on a regular basis, they were lifting up images of the passion, compassion, and courage reflected in the lives, and sometimes deaths, of those soldiers whose primary commitments on the battlefield and elsewhere have been to *ahimsa* (nonviolence) and the *satyagraha* (truthforce) in their lives. Many soldiers past and present have been rooted in this sacred power, men and women warriors who have lived and died truly in the service of compassion and peace. Most communities could lift up images of such young and older soldiers whose ways of being in the world, including battle, have been rooted and grounded in a struggle for peace and mercy. Christian churches would make a creative contribution to the world if they were to find ways of publicly celebrating the courage of these good warriors who are among the saints of God, men and women who have loved and respected their enemies rather than simply hating, fighting, and killing them.

In his own work, Gandhi came to realize that some warriors, often the bravest and most compassionate, those whose roots had grown most deeply in *satyagraha,* began to seek nonviolence as a way of life not only for themselves but also for the world. For these good warriors, nonviolence became not only a personal goal but also a social and political aim and a strategy for bringing about social change. Through his association with these good warriors, Gandhi increasingly realized that *nonviolent resistance* — both a deeply personal struggle and a radical social movement — requires the courage of a warrior to fight and if need be die; but he realized also that it takes the courage of nonviolent resisters and other peace-builders, a courage to be ridiculed, to stand out among peers as "weird," to be branded "unpatriotic," "treasonous" — and, in these times, a "supporter of terrorism."

Building peace, or making nonviolence, requires passion — in the double sense of having both a zest for life and justice and a willingness to suffer on behalf of this passion. It also requires compassion not only for victims of violence but also for those who wage war and inflict violence, because war-makers often do not know what they are doing. They believe they are doing what is right and necessary in the service of a higher good — like freedom and democracy (if they are fighters for the United States), or like the strengthening of Islam (if they are fighters for Al Qaeda).

A spiritually weak person does not have the moral strength to be a warrior for peace. Such a good warrior must be vulnerable — open to personal suffering and to compassion, "suffering with" others. If Christians honestly believe that all humans are called to live in, and as, the image of God, we can hear a shared call to live in the image of a good warrior God, a courageous Spirit of vulnerability to suffering and compassion in the ongoing struggles against violence and other forms of evil.

The Question of Sacrifice

Must we then be willing, as Jesus suggested, to lay down our lives for our friends, our country, and our God as we understand God? And if so, how do we distinguish between a "good sacrifice" and the suicidal act of the nineteen hijackers on September 11? Mohamed Atta and his comrades evidently believed they were following the dictates of Allah on that fateful day, much as most Christians have believed that Jesus was following the will of his Father when he went willingly to his death on the cross. What is the difference between these two images of sacrifice?

The most obvious difference is that the terrorist bombers not only "sacrificed" themselves but thousands of other people who had no choice in the matter.

It is surely possible for a person to make a holy and living sacrifice of himself or herself. History is full of such examples: the monk who immolates himself on behalf of peace, the driver who swerves off the road to avoid hitting someone else, the camp counselor who dies trying to save a child from falling over a cliff, the passengers on Flight 93 on September 11, the many instances of soldiers who have suffered death themselves rather than kill people whom they perceived to be innocent. To allow oneself to suffer and die to save someone else, or in someone else's place, is a primary example of the Love that is God that is *satyagraha,* the most sacred and foundational "soul-force" imaginable.

But to sacrifice *others'* lives, even if on behalf of what we believe to be God's will, is *never* a spiritually good or moral option. The September 11 hijackers, however sincere in their belief that they were being faithful to Allah, were not faithful to Allah or to any other image of a God of Love and Mercy, Justice and Compassion.

But what if these nineteen young men, the suicide bombers, believed that killing of thousands of people was the only way to get the world's attention and, thereby, to set in motion a process — a war — that would eventually save the lives of millions of poor Muslims throughout the world? If this was perhaps their motive, how is this different from the U.S. war against terrorism, which may be requiring the slaughter of hundreds or thousands of individuals no less "innocent" than those going about their lives in the World Trade Center, the Pentagon, and the four airliners on September 11?

What makes one war evil and another good if each is waged in a belief that it is being fought in order to save "innocent" people, be they poor Muslims in Arab nations or United States citizens going about their daily business? I think the difference — which usually can be seen only in historical perspective — is the extent to which any war effort is genuinely waged on behalf of saving and liberating others rather than destroying or controlling them, together with the real efforts of soldiers to exercise compassion and mercy whenever and wherever possible.

To sacrifice the lives of *others* is evil. This is what war is about, always and inevitably. We sacrifice other people. In this important sense, war is evil, all war — "their" wars and "our" wars, wars past and wars present, even "good wars" like those against Hitler, Pol Pot, Idi Amin, and now this war against terrorism.

War is evil because it requires the sacrifice of lives other than one's own (or along with one's own); but also because it generates spirals of violence that span generations, giving violence a forceful impetus in history, and often one held "sacred" by religious people. On every continent, violence generates violence, sacrifice sparks sacrifice, evil begets evil, sons and daughters inherit their parents' legacies of destruction and death, however noble or courageous the elders' individual lives may have been. Wars leave legacies of hatred and sometimes love as well.

But can such love as that manifested by a compassionate soldier ever really transcend the hatred and bitterness that shaped its context? War provides countless occasions for courage, compassion, and love to shine forth, and for heroes to rise up from the rubble of horror and despair. But war is first and foremost a campaign of death and destruction. The violence and evil that it both spawns and sets in motion can never be undone by the courage and love of those "good warriors" whose lives and deaths may reflect brilliantly the image of God.

Even though war is evil, there will always be a place for the good warrior, divine and human, in the theological imagination as well as in the midst of life. In the real world in which someone is always at war, there will be an important moral place for the warrior who struggles for peace, the soldier who exercises compassion, the fighter who earnestly desires nonviolence as a way of life. The values of the good warrior reflect the moral life to which all of us are called — to fight if need be, perhaps even to kill if we must and can, but to be always seeking ways to wage peace and always learning what it means to love our enemies as ourselves. A "good soldier" may be the best teacher of enemy-love.

Christians can look to Jesus as someone who loved his enemies and who sacrificed his life rather than submit to the powers of evil in history as he experienced them. So they killed him, these principalities and powers of the state. Jesus did not take others with him to death nor did he destroy them along the way. To the contrary, he spent his entire life, as far as we can tell, restoring others to life, helping others tap resources for personal healing and sowing seeds among them for social transformation and liberation. By living as a lover of sisters and brothers and of the God whom he experienced as working with and through himself and others, Jesus stirred great fear among the secular and religious keepers of law and order. This is why they killed him — they were afraid of him, afraid of his charisma among the people, afraid of his little movement of God-lovers. So they forced him to choose between saving himself and being true to himself by continuing to trust *satyagraha,* the soul-force/God of his life. Given this choice, Jesus chose to be true to himself and his God. This is when they hung him on the tree.

We need to be clear that Jesus went to Calvary and his death not in obedience to a God who required, much less desired, such a human sacrifice but rather because he was attempting to live deeply in *satyagraha,* desiring to be true to himself, his sisters and brothers, and the Holy One who, Jesus knew, did not desire sacrifice. The Hebrew scriptures, Jesus' own spiritual reference, make clear that God desires "steadfast love and not sacrifice, the knowledge of God rather than burnt offerings" (Hos. 6:6). "To do righteousness and justice is more acceptable to [God] than sacrifice" (Prov. 21:3).

What happened to Jesus on the cross was not God's sacrifice of Jesus. Nor was it "God's will." It was a consequence of human sin and evil. God did not crucify Jesus. His death was schemed and executed by the social and political powers of the Roman Empire. Jesus was a victim of the structures of domination and violence under which he and others lived. These principalities and powers crucified him — just as they crucified thousands of people on September 11 and also many Afghani shopkeepers and herdspeople who died in the early months of the war against terrorism.

Holy Communion: What Are We Celebrating?

Christianity for the most part has taught that the Eucharist (Greek for "thanksgiving") is a celebration of Jesus Christ's sacrifice on the cross for the sins of the world. This is true, and yet profoundly misleading. Jesus died on the cross *because of* the sins of the world. The world killed Jesus just as it has countless women and men throughout history, people of all religious and cultural traditions who in various ways represent a threat to the established order. In that sense Jesus died "for the sins of the world." But Jesus' death did not, as most Christian orthodoxy has claimed, take away the world's sin or in any way remove the problems of sin (alienation from God) and evil (structures of violence rooted in sin). Sin and evil are as real and threatening today as they ever were. The cross did not, and does not, eliminate them. We Christians fool ourselves at great spiritual and moral cost to ourselves and others if we imagine that, because Jesus died on the cross, the spiritual problem of our ongoing involvement in sin and evil has been erased by God.

What happened on the cross was not — and is not — so simple. We need to remember, first, that "the cross" represents *any* infliction of unjust punishment, suffering, or death on human or other creatures. The Christian cross does not signify primarily a past event, but rather the *ongoing* problem of evil in history. What happened to Jesus is what often happens to good people in the world — good warriors, good parents, and all who are committed to struggling for mutuality and nonviolence as ways of life in a world in which structures of domination and violence seem almost always to have the upper hand.

For Christians, the cross does not stand alone as a sign of salvation or liberation. We celebrate a spiritual "event" that includes both Jesus' crucifixion and his resurrection. And the resurrection is not primarily a miracle or a supernatural occurrence. The resurrection was the refusal by Jesus' community of friends to let his death destroy his presence and power among them. Resurrection is a radical affirmation of the ongoingness of life that transforms any community of people who refuse, through the power of faith, to let the power of any one's love be destroyed.

Jesus' crucifixion and resurrection, together, have become for many Christians a sign and a promise that God's power working through Jesus and his friends was, is, and will be forever stronger than the power of evil in the world. By the power of God, the force of love and compassion rises above death on the cross. This is as real today as it was when Jesus himself was executed. This is the sense in which sin and evil are defeated by the cross and empty tomb. Love is simply stronger than fear.

It is not then that the blood of the cross washes away the sins of the world, but rather that the sacred power of resurrection breaks the spiral of violence and evil — and shows us what is possible, through faith. Indeed, the one who dies now lives! In this resurrection faith, we experience the burden of fear lifted from us, again and again, as we ourselves are en-couraged morning by morning and day by day.

But what of the strange notion, long standing in mainstream Catholic and Protestant Christianity, that Jesus' death was, in some legal sense, a payment for human sin; that his death was "required" by God because of "the sins of the world"? As Christian feminists have indicated repeatedly over the last several decades, such a distortion of God's love is a shameful theological teaching that can be, and unfortunately is, used around the world to justify child abuse and other forms of violence exercised by "fathers," "masters," and other rulers against subordinates, who imagine that they are acting in the image of such a God, who truly is a God of Terror.

We need to reject any understanding of the Eucharist as a rite of thanksgiving for such a God of Terror, a Father who would "sacrifice" his Son and who would "require" Jesus' death on the cross in our sinful place. This line of theological reasoning is unfaithful to a God who is the Spirit of Love, Jesus' *abba*/Father, the Creator of all that is most just and compassionate. And this is the One whom we truly can affirm in our prayers of eucharistic thanksgiving — the God who is the *satyagraha* that we Christians encounter through the story of Jesus and through his ongoing spiritual presence with us even now, a brother, our spiritual kin, one who has gone on before us into the larger realm of the Spirit. It is this God, whom we glimpse through the witness of Jesus in relation to God and to sisters and brothers, for whom we give thanks in the eucharistic celebration.

And so we are not celebrating Jesus' sacrificial death on the cross except as a dimension of a life well-lived in the Sacred Spirit. In the Eucharist, we give thanks most basically for Jesus' life and his ongoing presence with us as brother and friend. We give thanks that, through Jesus' witness, we are better able to recognize and give thanks to the God whom we encounter in one another and in all others — those whom we know, those whom we do not know; those who remind us of ourselves, those whose cultures and ways are foreign to us; those who are Christian and people of other faith traditions; those of us who are human and those who are creatures-other-than-human. In the Eucharist, we celebrate the Holy Spirit, whose presence infuses the created world and urges human history in directions of justice and compassion.

In this marvelous spiritual context, we celebrate the power of love, human and divine, in which a brother gives up, lets go of, his own life rather than betray himself, other humans, and the God whom he loved. In this sense Jesus sacrificed himself. As a good mother, God does not sacrifice her children; as a good father, God did not sacrifice Jesus.

There is a sense, however, in which through Jesus' willingness to die, *God was sacrificing Godself.* Let me explain. In any human life, God — the Spirit of Love — is at the core of a person's willingness to give up her own life, not others' lives, in order to be true to herself and her God. In this sense, God was sacrificing Godself through Jesus' death on the cross. Through this image of God's own self-relinquishment, Christians are met with an image of a radically vulnerable God as our highest power, a Spirit open to suffering and death at the hands of an unjust world. Is this not a powerful image of God as good Father, good Mother, good warrior, a good friend who is willing to lay down her life for those whom she loves? It is a strong image of *satyagraha,* the truth-force that we gather to lift up and give thanks for each time we share the Eucharist and make our Holy Communion.

For most Christians, Jesus of Nazareth is "Christ," a term derived from the Greek, which means "messiah," "anointed one," or "savior." We name him Christ because through his life, death, and resurrection, we — like those who have gone before us — are drawn into a collective and personal experience of salvation, an experience of being rescued from drowning in overwhelming depths of fear, grief, and anger that, left spiritually unattended, can so easily become despair and hatred turned against ourselves and others.

Because I believe so strongly that Jesus' power was, and is, sacred only because it is shared — a power for generating mutual healing and liberation — I am among those Christians who seek other ways of imaging Jesus' relation to the rest of us. One such way is to speak of the "christic power" sparked in history by Jesus and his small movement of friends and disciples. The terms "christic power" and "Holy Spirit" refer to the same sacred energy, the same love, the same God. They are particularly Christian terms for a real presence — God, our power in mutual relation — that is not, and cannot be, and does not seek to be, exclusively Christian.

The liturgical eucharistic image of "the body of Christ" that is "broken for us" refers to Jesus' gift of himself — his giving himself over to death rather than betraying himself and his God. But the body of Christ refers to more than Jesus' body — it points to the body of humanity and the body of all creation groaning for God, yearning for *satyagraha*. And the body of Christ is more than the body of humanity and creation. It is also God's body in the context of our struggles to love one another and our openness to God's presence and guidance in these struggles.

Thus, in Holy Communion, we gather to celebrate ourselves, one another, and the Spirit that we meet through one another's love, advocacy, and compassion. We give thanks for Jesus, for God, and for one another — including ourselves — as lovers of God and the world. This is what the Eucharist is all about. Through faith, the body and blood of Christ become spiritual food and drink that nourish us to live faithfully in *satyagraha*.

Through the Eucharist, we are empowered to live as warriors for peace, as mothers and fathers to a needy world, as sons and daughters of a Mother-Father God whose very essence is to encourage us, and as friends to one another in the ongoing struggles to create a more fully just and compassionate world. More than anything, we are encouraged to recognize ourselves as Jesus' sisters and brothers — and Jesus as one of us, with us in the balance between such evils as war and patriarchy, racism and violence, on the one hand and, on the other, the realm of Spirit in which courageous warriors beat swords into plowshares. In this realm men give up patriarchal power as they learn to live in mutual partnership with women and each other. This is the kin-dom of God in which we realize that God is not so much a power over us as the *satyagraha* in which we live and breathe and have our being.

Too Late for Peace?

Until the bombing of Afghanistan began, many of us were hoping that the United States would find a way to exercise more restraint in the "war against terrorism." We had hoped that a well-considered nonviolent plan — freezing of assets, building a global coalition, using all available international venues of justice — might constitute a forceful, quite possibly effective, response to the horrific events of September 11. After all, the bombing of buildings with passenger jets was such a mighty evil that nothing less than the most forceful response our government could make has been morally thinkable. No doubt this is why most people in the U.S. seem to agree that a military response to the terrorist attack was necessary. We have begun waging a war that we probably can win someday. But can we win it violently without destroying the very people we hope to save, including ourselves?

Is it too late for us to wage peace? It is not too late for us, as a nation, to commit ourselves to peace-building even when it would require, as it would, an effort by the United States to begin rebuilding what has been destroyed over decades by our bombs, our guns, and our long-standing reputation in much of the world as a nation that does not know how to wage peace. Vietnam and the Persian Gulf, the contra forces in Nicaragua and the Bay of Pigs in Cuba — these and other instances of our war machine may seem remote and disconnected from the current crisis, but they are not. Outside the United States,

---

This chapter was first published in the *Asheville Citizen-Times* on November 4, 2001, A-9, 10, under the title, "Is It Too Late to Commit Ourselves to Peace Building?"

most people are appalled by the terrorist attacks on our country and, at the same time, are puzzled that so many of us do not seem able to connect what has happened with our country's international reputation for stirring violence wherever it suits us.

Is it not time now to reverse this course and use our power for peacemaking? Indeed, peace should be not only the goal of the war on terrorism. Peacemaking as an active commitment to nonviolence should become the way we move toward this goal. Let us be clear: nonviolence does *not* mean that we sit back and do nothing if, for example, we are on a plane that is being hijacked. To the contrary, we do whatever we can to foil the hijacking. Nonviolent resistance means that, in any violent situation, we *do everything possible to stop the violence*. It also means that we try if at all possible to respect the humanity of our enemies.

The journalist Andrew Sullivan has suggested that the U.S. Constitution is our most potent weapon against bin Laden and his network of true believers in a distortion of Islam that scorns the very notion of peacemaking with "infidels." Guided by the Constitution, which protects our rights to such freedoms as speech, religion, and association, the United States, if we were to become a global peacemaker, would join in an international peace-building movement dedicated to liberty and justice for all, within and beyond our national boundaries.

This, of course, is the purpose of the United Nations, which was acknowledged recently when the UN and its Secretary General Kofi Annan were named recipients of the Nobel Peace Prize. Is it not time for the United States to lay aside its petulant resistance to UN leadership and join other nations in mounting a strong movement against terrorism that we here at home as well as our sisters and brothers throughout the Middle East and elsewhere in the world can truly live with?

Ironically, when so much evil has been done throughout history in the name of God, there are hallowed traditions of peace and nonviolent resistance in each of the world's major religions. We are in urgent need today for leadership from the sacred traditions of nonviolence, especially though not only from Christians, Muslims, and Jews. We who are religious leaders ourselves must start speaking publicly of peace and teaching peace as a way of life, spirituality, and politics. We need to use newspapers, television, religious organizations, schools, workplaces, cultural centers, and the streets to spread the word that nonviolent resistance is the only force in human history that, in the long run, is stronger than bombs and more cunning than terrorism.

Here in the United States right now, it is unpopular to advocate nonviolent resistance. Yet we religious leaders must do exactly that. We must voice our dissent in a national culture that is warning us that "good Americans" must be in favor of war. It is probably more important than ever for us to be insisting upon political space for dissent and opposition in the United States. After all, is it not our enemy who represents the reign of terror in which there is no space for opposition and no permission for dissent?

A nonviolent international struggle against terrorism, an effort inspired by an interfaith coalition of nonviolent religious traditions, would become a massive effort to open up space: political and social space, cultural and spiritual space, psychological and physical space for people to be themselves amid multiple varieties and styles of human being. Such forceful resistance to terrorism would be steeped in recognition of our differences, tolerance of the tensions among us, and faith that the ambiguities we embody can be creative teachers rather than demons to damn us.

It is time to stop sneering at those who call for peace. We need rather to be lifting up leaders like Rep. Barbara Lee (D-Cal.), who cast the only vote in Congress against the military assault on terrorism. Representative Lee knows what Desmond Tutu, Martin Luther King Jr., Mahatma Gandhi, and Jesus of Nazareth knew — that nonviolent resistance not only is the strongest way; it is the only way to a lasting peace.

Far from being a fluffy-brained notion, nonviolence demands shrewd political strategies as well as radical, life-changing spiritual commitments. In the final analysis, hand in hand with our Constitution, spiritualities of nonviolence are likely to be the United States' most effective weapons against terrorism.

Part Two

God as Father
and
God as Spirit

തൈക്കൈക്കൈക്കൈ

Our Father, who art in heaven,
hallowed be thy name.
Thy kingdom come, thy will be done
on earth as it is in heaven.
Give us this day our daily bread.
And forgive us our trespasses,
as we forgive those who trespass against us.
And lead us not into temptation,
but deliver us from evil.
For thine is the kingdom,
and the power, and the glory,
forever and ever. Amen.

THREE

Transforming the Father

From all reports, Christians began flocking back to church after September 11, 2001. Although this seems to have been an early response to the events and not, for many Christians, a lasting one, it nonetheless said something about the spiritual impact of that day. Grief and fear are powerful spiritual motivators, and many of us have been deeply in grief since the attacks, whether or not we lost personal friends and colleagues in them. Our grief has been not only for the lives destroyed but also for the shattering of whatever illusion we may have had of the United States as, in any simple way, a safe or easy place to live or perhaps (dare I suggest?) an unambiguously good place to call home.

In addition to being grief-stricken, most people in the United States have been profoundly frightened by these events. Most of us — especially white people — are not used to living under the threat of something so big and terrible, something we cannot control or even recognize among us. The image of the second plane flying into the World Trade Center is probably etched forever in our minds. As many noted at the time, it seemed like a movie. But it wasn't, and it isn't. We are, for real, living in a world and a country in which the God of Terror is competing for our allegiances and our lives. It seems that we are not only "standing in the need of prayer" but, more than before, many of us *know* we are. So we turned, at least for awhile, back to our mosques, temples, meeting houses, centers of meditation, prayer circles, and churches.

Faith of Our Fathers

When Christians get to church, we are greeted in the name of God the Father and of his Son Jesus and of the Holy Spirit. For most Christians this greeting brings a sense of comfort and of being at home. For some of us, while it may bring some comfort and security, it also brings frustration and a sense of being left out. The "faith of our fathers" represents for us a spiritual ambivalence and confusion. We know in our bones that Christianity bears much wisdom but also seeds of terror and violence done to others "in the name of Christ." In this particular moment in history, as we stagger in renewed awareness of how deadly a patriarchal religious tradition can be, many Christians (like Muslim, Jewish, and other sisters and brothers) are seeking to lift up the wisdom, the healing and peace-building resources, in our traditions. For either these life-affirming currents will show themselves stronger than the death-dealing tides of terror, or we must be done with these religious traditions. Speaking for myself, I can no longer reverence icons of patriarchal power unless they are undergoing a radical spiritual transformation in our worship and our lives. And this will happen only if you and I, the Spirit working through us, generate this reformation in Christian theology, worship, and life.

These reflections on the Father God in relation to the Spirit explore the possibility of liberating ourselves from a God made in the image of powerful men, liberating the Father from patriarchal Christianity, and taking small steps to begin to liberate Christianity from its moorings in male supremacy, an effort that will take many movements and lifetimes across cultures and continents.

At its best, the Father God tradition represents *the good parent* whose love for the child is nurturing: encouraging and protective, compassionate and forgiving, instructive and inspirational, never violent or harmful toward the child. This kind of parent is what the church over the years most often has intended to convey through its father-image, which is meant to reflect Jesus' experiences of God. But we need to remember that there is a difference between intent and impact. And regardless of intent, the impact of the theological image of Father has been shaped historically by patriarchy.

Let me be clear what I mean by "patriarchy." It is the organization of society around the special rights and privileges of men in general, fathers in particular, and especially men and fathers of the ruling classes, to control the lives of everyone in the society. As a patriarchal sign, which is how it has functioned throughout Christian history, the term "Father" is less about Jesus' experience of God than about Christian men's experiences of power over women and children — a power to name, rule, and judge; to punish, reward, and determine outcomes; to exercise vengeance or mercy. In a patriarchal society, to pray to God the Father is never simply to reach out personally to a God whom we experience, or yearn for, as a loving protective parent, which is no doubt what most of us are praying for in these times of fear and grief. Regardless, however, of our intent, our prayer — especially if it is public and corporate, as it is when we are in church — plays a role in upholding patriarchal power relations. What are we to make of this?

Jesus' Experience of His Father

Let's begin with an acknowledgment of Jesus' experience of God, which seems to have been like a son's experience of a father (Matt. 7:21, 10:32; Mark 14:36; Luke 11:2, 22:29). In the Jesus stories as recorded in Christian scripture, Jesus is rooted and grounded in God, the son rooted and grounded in the father. From his Father God, Jesus receives the spiritual energy to live for the neighbor, to heal, to teach, to bear God's love in the world. It's as if the Father God is the soil and the son Jesus is the plant.

Elsewhere I have suggested that, in the Spirit of mutuality — which truly is the Holy Spirit — Jesus also grounds God in human history; and God, like a child, grows in the world through Jesus' life and witness. In any case, the Father-Son relationship — if it is a good one, which clearly Christians believe that it was, and is, between God and Jesus — is a *relationship of mutual nurturance,* just as it would be if it were a Mother and child, son or daughter. The parent provides grounding, direction, and comfort (another word for a sense of strengthening); and the child also grounds, directs, and strengthens the parent's presence in the community and world.

We must be clear that the resistance among Christians to experiencing the Motherhood of God reflects the stranglehold of patriarchal consciousness on Christian faith. The resistance to naming, worshiping, and learning to love God the Mother has nothing to do with the life and witness of Jesus, who repeatedly rejected narrow-minded, literalist interpretations of religious law and custom in favor of living in the Spirit of openness to human need and inclusion of those left out. And is it not Jesus whose life is, for Christians, a primary window into God?

As a Christian theologian, teacher, and priest, I've been wrestling with experiences and images of Jesus for about forty years. Even as a teenager, I tried to make sense of many white Episcopalians' resistance to the civil rights movement. There were exceptions, of course, like John Hines, the presiding bishop, and the eloquent layman and lawyer William Stringfellow. Wouldn't Jesus want us to be out there marching like these bold individuals? More to the point, wasn't Jesus himself out there among the marchers and folks sitting in at the lunch counters? Wasn't Martin Luther King Jr. himself not only a disciple of Jesus but, in some very real sense, an embodiment of Jesus for us in our own time and place in history? Weren't all those marchers for justice and human rights embodying, and manifesting, "christic power," the same power of God that sparked the life of Jesus? These were some of my questions in my teens and early twenties, stated here in the theological language of my forties and fifties.

Our Image of God the Father

Over the years, through involvement in various justice movements as well as ongoing participation in the church, seminary
teaching, and broad-based ecumenical and interfaith movements in religious feminism and feminist liberation theologies,
I have come to believe that Jesus of Nazareth was one of us,
a human brother on this earth. Through his life we are able
to recognize the Spirit of God as the power generating and
struggling for mutual relation among us collectively and individually. I have believed strongly that this sacred power in the
struggle for mutual relation is the God whom Jesus knew and
loved as an *abba* (father); and that when we Christians pray
to "Our Father," we are actually invoking this divine, spirited
energy for mutuality in all arenas of our life together. Not
that this is what most Christians think they are doing, because
most Christians are educated to mistake literalism for faith,
and law for Spirit, which Jesus himself warned against (Mark
2:23–3:6; Matt. 12:1–14).

For this reason, like many Christian women and some men
as well, I have been troubled in my soul by the monopoly
that God the Father has held in most Christian worship. My
discomfort has been stirred by the extent to which Christian
leaders, even many of the most progressive women and men —
by the constancy of their public invocation of the Father —
continue to uphold patriarchal standards and, thereby, contribute to violence against women and children and to false
teachings about God as well as human beings and other creatures. That this is not the intention of most Christian leaders
suggests that they do not grasp the power of liturgy to shape
lives. Or perhaps it is simply that they have become spiritually
depressed and are resigned to making peace with oppression,
their own and others'.

I might not intend to contribute to white supremacy in
teaching a basic course in Christian theology that draws
exclusively on the experiences and contributions of white Euro-

americans, but the impact of such a course would be to perpetuate future church leaders' assumptions that the best and brightest Christian theologians are white. These assumptions play into the perpetuation of white supremacy in church and society. So too with the monopoly of father imagery for God. Despite the intentions of many good men and women, the invocation of God the Father as the primary and often only image of God in Christian worship contributes to the ongoing diminishment of women and girls.

For this reason, several generations of feminist and womanist theologians have been trying to help the churches move "beyond God the Father" as the one and only gendered image for the God whom Jesus loved.[8] Because most churches have been so slow to welcome significant theological or liturgical change — especially to make God imagery more inclusive and, thereby, the worship of God more genuinely engaging for many women — large numbers of women have lost interest in the church over the past several decades. After all, why bother getting frustrated and resentful once a week? More importantly, do we want to contribute our time, energy, and gifts to the perpetuation of patriarchal religion? Such questions and the convictions that underlie them have prevailed among women who used to go to church but stopped somewhere along the way, preferring personal prayer, women's circles, and often other spiritual traditions like the Society of Friends, engaged Buddhism, or Wicca ("old" European traditions that predated Christianity among peoples like the Celts).

Beyond September 11 and God the Father

The post–September 11 world has seen quite a few Christian feminists returning to worship alongside many others who have come back to pray together in the midst of a crisis that we realize is as spiritual as it is political. Sitting in church services during the fall of 2001 myself, I became deeply mindful of the power of God the Father to draw us to him in times of grief, fear, and anger. Regardless of our personal experiences with fathers (and mine were wonderful, as good as they get), and whether we are five or eighty-five, most of us share a longing for an ongoing experience of good fathering and mothering, as well as to be good parents if we have children.

Long before the current crisis in the United States, I had come to realize that it is pointless to try to imagine a Christianity without a Father God. I pretty much had resigned myself to his ubiquitous control and, for the sake of conscience and sanity, had placed myself on the margins of Christian worship. But the aftermath of the terrorist attack has helped me see more clearly what many of my African American Christian sisters have known all along — that any effort to eliminate God the Father as an important spiritual image would be not only futile but also a bad idea pastorally, because many Christians need and desire his presence.

The war on terrorism also has begun to clarify for me how morally and politically unnecessary it is to try to dispense with or avoid Father God imagery. The theological image of God as Father not only means a great deal to most Christians; much of what it means is positive and life-giving. Along with their experiences of Jesus Christ, God the Father is the mainstay of their faith.

Now, to be sure, the term "Father" is a sign of patriarchy that continues to play a major part in the oppression of women and girls throughout the world and church. Because this is so, I believe the better part of Christian feminist wisdom is not to try to disengage people from this patriarchal image but rather to help lead the church in transforming the Father. What is at stake here is too important for us to turn our backs on. If most Christians experience God the Father as a source of personal hope and many as a resource for political courage as well, imagine how much more liberating the Father might become if he were being transformed into a nonsexist, liberating energy for mutuality!

So my theological question about God the Father has become not, how do we get rid of him? but rather, how can we continue to worship him without supporting patriarchy, sexism, heterosexism, and the many economic, political, and psychological ills bound up in these violent social structures? My sister philosopher Mary Daly would no doubt say that I have lost it here. Indeed for thirty years, she and I have differed in our understandings not so much of the debilitating character of patriarchy in women's lives but of whether, in our own time and place in history, we can shake the foundations of Christianity with enough woman-affirming energy to transform them. Mary Daly says that we cannot and, even if we could, why bother? I disagree with her about this and believe that, for many Christians, it's more of an opportunity than a "bother" (though often it is that as well!) to plod along together as agents of theological, spiritual, and social change.

The key to our being able to work in this way is in experiencing ourselves together, in movement and process, rather than as alone, disconnected from our sisters and brothers. This is why books, stories, pictures, films, songs, and other resources that can be shared and passed around, often literally around the world, are so vital to Euroamerican feminist, womanist, Chicana, Asian, African, and other Christian women. Such resources help us realize that, even in parts of the nation and world in which we're lonely for companions in the struggle, we're not alone. By the power of the woman-loving Spirit, we're in this together.

Let me say it again: there are no unchangeable dimensions of Christianity, a religion founded and organized by human beings just like us. To the extent that it is a peoples' religion — and we must insist that it is the faith of a people who experience God's presence with us here on the earth — we are responsible for continuing to reinterpret and revitalize the essence of Christianity itself. Indeed, we can transform not merely the surface of Christian tradition but its roots. This is because no part of our past — no single interpretation of the Bible, no religious doctrine, no theme in our history as a people — is fastened in spiritual cement.

Experiencing ourselves as participants in a religion that, like all religions, is best understood as a work-in-progress, can we begin to think differently about the theological image of God the Father? Can we Christians begin to imagine that we *can* love and worship a Father God — but *only* as he becomes increasingly a force for inclusivity, mutuality, and nonviolence among us? By "us" I mean not only Christian women and children, but also Christian men. I also mean people who are not Christian and the rest of creation as well, the other-than-human creatures.

We can be sure that God the Father will not be transformed in this way unless we are relentless in our insistence. And this, I suggest, is our bounden duty, our spiritual vocation as God-loving women and men, to be exactly that — adamant, persistent, and patient in our insistence that the Father give up all claims to be the only, best, or highest image of God; that he renounce violence and coercion as creative ways of being God; and that he let go of any notion that his "divinity" (the essence of his god-ness) derives from subordinates who obey him.

Am I speaking here of God in the fullness of God's own being or, a bit more modestly, of our experiences and perceptions of God? I could not speak with such bold confidence about the essence of a God Spirit that lives and moves and has its being way beyond not only this world but also our capacities to imagine, much less comprehend. I am happy, however, to speak theologically about human organizations like the Christian church and our experiences, perceptions, understandings, and images of God. For, however inspired, all theology — including Christian scriptures — is rooted in human experiences and perceptions.

Why this is so hard for many Christians in the United States and Europe to accept used to puzzle me. Over time, I have come to realize the extent to which Christian faith has been used by many people as an escape hatch from our most genuinely human experiences, including most of our deepest emotions. The fact is: if God is truly with us — fathering, mothering, and befriending us; nurturing, comforting, challenging, and struggling with us — then our experiences of God teach us about God. This is how the Bible came to be. It is how the most reliable spiritual testimonies have always been forged — in the crucibles of human experience.[9]

For us to insist, therefore, that the Father must give up claims of being the only, best, or highest image of God is a way of saying that *we Christians, we who are the church, must give up our perceptions of God the Father as the only, best, or highest image of God.* For it will always be our views, our words, our ways of imaging and thinking about God that create and constitute Christian faith. This has been true from the beginning. God is above and beyond us, beneath and behind our perceptions and understandings, including my writing and your reading this book. As a Christian, I am confident that God doesn't give a whit what we call her or how we image him as long as we are doing justice and loving mercy and walking humbly with our God (Mic. 6:8).

And so we proceed. But how are we to know what the Father must become? On the basis of what authority am I proposing that he become a more fully inclusive, nonviolent power for making mutual relation? Moreover, on the basis of what spiritual responsibility do you and I join in this process of theological transformation?

Our Image of God as Spirit

The answer to these questions is simple. It is by the power of the Holy Spirit that we ask these questions and undertake this reformation. We work in the Spirit that is writing and speaking, learning and teaching, through us, even in the pages of this little book. We teach in the Spirit of God on the basis of what the Spirit is teaching us about ourselves, God, and the world.

In patriarchal Christianity, *the Spirit lives and breathes in creative tension with the Father.* She pulls against him. She wrestles with him. She challenges him. She grounds him. Without her, God the Father is merely a spiritual relic — stale, brittle, often violent, sometimes terrorist. With and in the Spirit, and only in the Spirit, can the Father be an image of the living God. Without the Spirit, the Father can be nothing good.

But who or what is this Spirit? In Christian tradition, the Holy Spirit is the ongoing presence of God in the world. Perhaps the most often cited biblical reference to the Spirit is the famous passage from Isaiah that Jesus quotes, in part, at the outset of his own ministry:

> "The spirit of the Lord GOD is upon me,
> because the LORD has anointed me;
> he has sent me to bring good news to the oppressed,
> to bind up the brokenhearted,
> to proclaim liberty to the captives,
> and release to the prisoners;
> to proclaim the year of the LORD's favor,
> and the day of vengeance of our God;
> to comfort all who mourn..."
>
> (Isa. 61:1–2; see also Luke 4:16–20
> and Matt. 11:5)

Throughout the Bible, the Spirit of God is described in many ways, most of them comforting. However, in the prophetic context of God's ever present struggle against evils of injustice and oppression, the Spirit can be fierce and threatening. In biblical times and later, the Spirit of God is basically experienced and portrayed as a free spirit, creative, liberating, and an ongoing source of blessing. She is the eternal movement of God throughout history. She is the "Holy Ghost" or "Holy Spirit," traditional English terms, I suggest, for what Gandhi named *satyagraha.*

I'm using the feminine pronoun "she" for the Spirit both to honor the Hebrew word for spirit, *ruach,* which is feminine, and also to help place the Spirit in tension with the Father, which is one of the places in our common life in which we need her to be — helping keep us in the balance between images of male and female strength.

Father-Spirit Tensions and Energies

To focus theologically on the tension between Spirit and Father is to participate in an ancient Christian tension between God-images that often do not seem compatible. While the Father-image often conveys a hierarchical relationship of authority and obedience,[10] the image of Spirit more often reflects the power of participation, friendship, and mutuality. The tension between experiences of Father and Spirit was formative in the first centuries of the church and provided much spiritual energy for the early church councils that produced statements of shared faith, such as the Nicene Creed. Though few Christian theologians, pastors, or priests acknowledge this, the Spirit that went into the formation of the historic creeds is much more important than the words of the creeds themselves.

Through our liturgies and lives, we can convey the energy and tension, the liveliness and creativity, that constitute the basis of a living faith. This is where Christian reformers belong today — with Jesus our brother, in the balance between Father and Spirit, each experience touching and transforming the other.

The Father opens up and becomes a more fully inclusive image of guidance and comfort, just as the Spirit becomes grounded, again and again, in particular stories and faith traditions — including the stories and traditions of patriarchal Christianity, within which she has an important creative and liberating role to play. The Spirit enables the Father to "cross over" — transcend — boundaries of gender, so that he can become the Mother or the Mother-Father or some other wonderfully imaginative transgendered power that includes us all, and all of us "crossing over" in our own senses of awareness and identity and relationship. In the Spirit or *satyagraha,* the Father-Mother God can transcend boundaries of age and become a child or boundaries of species and become a tree or an elephant. All of this can happen in the Spirit of God seeking mutuality, nonviolence, and inclusivity.

On each occasion, the Father's particular energy — as parent and comforter, creator and nurturer — grounds the boundary-breaking Spirit in a distinct and personal form and shape. And so we are able to hear and recognize the Spirit in the birdsong and the horse's nickering, in the child's laughter and the lover's sighs. We meet the Spirit in the prisoner and the poet, the clerk and the soldier. We see that he can be our Father, she can be our Mother, our Sister, our Brother, depending upon context, moment, and need — our need as well as the Spirit's need to be revealed, again and again, among us.

Recognizing ourselves as Jesus' sisters and brothers, Christian theologians become shapers of doctrine, discipline, and worship. We learn together how to sway and bend more confidently in the balance between past and future, exploring how the Spirited Father might be experienced and celebrated as an inclusive peacemaking power to generate mutual relation.

But now, a warning: Under the rules of patriarchal Christianity, there is little space for creative conversations like those I am hoping this book is sparking. Because they do not want to lose their institutional clout, those churchmen and women who hold patriarchal power in place often are committed to as little disruption of doctrinal and liturgical patterns as possible. In such a constrictive climate (I do not say "conservative" because this book is itself conservative in important ways), those who are calling for theological transformation are often rejected as heretical. More commonly in the modern and postmodern world, we are simply dismissed as ignorant, idealistic, or out of touch with the real world and church. Aware that we're likely to be ignored or criticized for our work, reformers need to be steeped in a passion for justice, self-confidence, good humor, and patience. We need to learn to take ourselves lightly even as we take this theological opportunity seriously. Whoever and wherever we are, we need also to be connected through networks of friendship and collegiality.

A Living Trinity

So where are we at this point in our study?

We see that the Father to whom so many Christians turned for comfort and protection in the wake of September 11 can become a transformed Father or Mother, a nurturing parent, rooted and grounded in the Holy Spirit of inclusivity, mutuality, and nonviolence.

We see that the Holy Spirit is the power that generates nonviolence, inclusivity, and mutuality.

We see that this Spirit is our source and resource for personal, social, political, and institutional transformation. And because she is our power for mutual relation, she is also being touched and transfigured all the time by those whom she touches, the changer and the changed.

And so we belong, with Jesus, in the balance between the steadfast Father that the church has passed on to us and the more radically inclusive, peacemaking Spirit or *satyagraha*.

For those interested in Christian doctrine, what is being proposed here is a living Trinity: Like Jesus, and in his memory and presence, you and I can live in the balance between our experiences of a nurturing Father/Mother God and a creative Spirit who is calling us to comfort the world, to be good parents and friends to a world which, in ways, is like a child — frightened and angry and spilling over with grief. And this "child," whom we share with sisters and brothers of many cultures and religions, does not need to be patronized. She needs our respect, friendship, and advocacy in the sacred Spirit of mutuality.

Beyond Shameful Theology

Christians everywhere must emphatically reject the theology of the Revs. Jerry Falwell, Pat Robertson, and other narrow-minded Christians who are inclined to interpret the terrible events of September 11 as God's judgment upon this nation or upon any group of people in it. As Episcopal Bishop Jane Holmes Dixon of Washington, D.C., has stated in the strongest possible terms, this theology is "beyond shameful." It has nothing to do with the love of God or Jesus of Nazareth. It also has nothing to do with Christian morality, which is about the deeply human struggles for right relation, not self-righteous judgments upon everybody except oneself and one's own.

We who are Christians, as well as people of other spiritual traditions such as Islam, Judaism, Buddhism, and Wicca, need to be clear and public in our shared affirmation of the Power of love in history. This Sacred Power, which most Christians call "God," heals the wounds that divide us. This God is a Spirit that "arcs toward justice," to quote the Rev. Irene Monroe, an African American theologian from Boston. In no way is this God ever involved in terrorist activities, except as God is deeply present with the victims and their loved ones.

The notion of a deity who violently wipes out his enemies is a terrible misinterpretation of Christian scripture with historic roots in our deep fear of "enemies" and in our very human inclination to make "God" in the image of this fear. The best

This chapter was first published in the *Charlotte Observer* on September 24, 2001, A-15, under the title, "Reject Falwell's Shameful Words."

that can be said about the Falwell-Robertson charge that —
due to the presence among us of feminists, lesbians, gay men,
abortionists, and other liberals — God chose not to "protect"
the United States from terrorism is that this spiritually ignorant
view reflects its proponents' own fears and moral confusion.
It would be simply a pathetic view if its proponents had not
become so politically influential over the last several decades.

As it is, the patriarchal theology of Falwell-Robertson has
become a political instrument of division and destruction being wielded against those whom they believe to be the enemies
of God. This weapon is being used not only in the name of a
judgmental and violent God but also, increasingly, in the name
of the United States of America. This theology of fear and
hate needs to be named for what it is: shameful and blasphe-
mous in relation to the God of love, justice, and compassion,
the One whom Jesus loved and the One whom Moses and
Mohammed also loved.

Especially chilling at this moment is the realization that the
Falwell-Robertson version of Christianity is a very close cousin
to the theology of those who bombed the World Trade Center
and Pentagon with hijacked commercial airliners. What we witnessed in horror as the planes hit their targets, taking with them
thousands of our brothers and sisters, was the dramatization
of a theology of fear, hatred, and narrow-minded absolutism
in which its proponents assumed that they, and they alone,
could speak for God and indeed represent God in the wiping
out of his enemies. Whether a perversion of Islam (as it seems
to have been in this case) or, in other instances, a perversion of
Judaism or Christianity, this wretched theology of judgment
and violence is a primary source of evil among us. In the name
of God, we must reject it.

So then what can be a loving and just response to Jerry
Falwell and other peddlers of this shameful stuff? This is an
important, ongoing question for Christians and others as well.
Its answers are neither clear nor simple, and we must pray for
the wisdom and courage to know how best to respond. But

I am sure that the most genuinely inspired responses have to do with learning how to love our enemies rather than simply attacking them, even as they attack us. Real love is justice-making with compassion. It poses a mighty spiritual challenge in these times to imagine what such enemy-love actually might require. But I also am sure that the justice-love of God is so vast, so broad, so high that it forever threatens to transform us — you and me, Jerry and Pat, other patriarchal religious leaders, even perhaps the terrorists who struck such a mighty blow to the heart of our nation.

Part Three

God in Us
and
God in All

೧೦ೂ೦ೂ೦ೂ೦ೂ

In the beginning when God created the heavens and the earth. . . .

And God said, "Let the earth bring forth living creatures of every kind: cattle and creeping things and wild animals of the earth. . . ."

Then God said, "Let us make humankind [*adam*] in our image, according to our likeness; and let them have dominion. . . ."

Genesis 1:1, 24, 26

ᥱᧁ FIVE ᧁᥱ

Creatures in the Image of (a Morally Complex) God

Along with tensions in the experiences of many Christians between Father and Spirit and between a Warrior deity and a God of peace comes, for many, the most elusive stress of all. I am referring to the pull between our belief in the "primacy" of human beings, who we believe are created in the image of God, and the sacred worth of the rest of creaturekind. Many Christians do not assume that creatures other than human also reflect the image of God. I am among those who do. I also believe that any lasting peace will involve the realization by people throughout the world of God's real presence *in* the rest of creation, not simply over it.

Dominion vs. Mutuality

But let's start at the beginning, with the dynamic that we humans have generated between our human selves and other creatures: a dynamic of domination and control. Our religious ancestors believed — as most Jews, Christians, and Muslims do today — that God has given humankind in general, males in particular, dominion or power over creation, and that this is a large part of what it means to be in the image of God. This perception of God's image and of ourselves in it was shaped by a patriarchal consciousness in which dominion and domination were primary images of sacred power, social order, and human responsibility.

More than ever we today need to be transforming this false and uncreative consciousness into an awareness that sacred, soulful power is not dominion. "Soul" has nothing to do with "power over." Far from it, divinity and the humanity created in its image is a Spirit of a radical mutuality that is constantly liberating and forever creative. Christian education, more than anything, should be a resource for social and personal transformation through the Spirit of mutual relation rather than simply another propagandistic system to help us cope with the dynamics of domination and submission upon which so much of our life together is constructed.

Now this is a point at which folks often will say to me, "This sounds nice, but it's totally unreal, this mutuality!" Interesting how many people, Christians and others, do not see that mutuality is, in fact, the basis of our life together in the cosmos. Mutuality is not a soft, sweet notion or a fluff-brain fantasy. Spiritually, physically, and socially, it's who we are. It's how we're constituted — radically interdependent and mutually interactive as humans with one another and with other creatures as well.

In my *Saving Jesus from Those Who Are Right*, I discussed what it means for us to be "mutual":

> The term "mutual" has a double... meaning, both metaphysical and ethical, mystical and moral. In the first place, "mutual" is almost synonymous with "relation." The white ash, the cat and I are mutually related... interconnected ecologically and economically, politically and spiritually, regardless of whether we notice.... In the second place, our moral work as human creatures is to notice this connectedness. We need to help one another learn how to participate in building a world in which the radically mutual basis of our life together will be noticed and desired, struggled for and celebrated. Ethically, the struggle for mutual relation becomes our life-commitment.[11]

Struggling for mutual relation is how we keep our balance. It is the "how to" of what it means to live in God. Far from being a sweet and easy thing, the building of mutuality is challenging moral, political, social, and psychological work. I've come to see that this is why religious and civic leaders so often trivialize and dismiss mutual relation and those of us who value it: Mutuality is a challenging goal for many people to imagine or even dare to desire! How much easier to exercise power over. How much less difficult to simply give over our spiritual authority to a bishop or priest and our political power to a king or president. How much more complicated to really share the power for shaping the world, the church, and other institutions. It is easier for most of us to hand over our power to others — divine and human others — and to allow them to exercise authority over us than it is for us, in Jesus' words, to "pick up our beds and walk" by learning to share power.

Yet the Christian vocation is to learn to experience God's power as shared power that belongs to no one alone, no Creator or creature alone, but rather to us all. This wonderfully transformative Christian spirituality roots our faith in God who is, at heart, the power for making and sustaining mutuality.

Nothing I am writing should be read as an invitation to romanticize human life or idealize God, ourselves, or nature. I am rather suggesting that we Christians help one another get clear about the radically interdependent character of all creation, in which we humans play significant, but never solo, roles in leadership.

I am also suggesting that sharing our power is what it means to be in the image of God and what it means to have "a soul." This is a spiritual vocation, a call from God, that many Christians have not yet heard. And yet it is a real call, a sacred call, a wake-up call from the earth, from the creatures of the earth and sky and sea, and from the people of the earth. It is a cry against dominion, a yearning for participation and involvement with one another across species as well as cultures, and a plea not simply for survival but as importantly, in Delores S. Williams's words, for "quality of life."[12] How then do we connect this "cry against dominion" to terrorism and the war against it?

A Cry for Mutuality?

There are two ways the terrorist attacks highlighted for me the
need for a Christian theology and politic of mutuality. First,
there was, and continues to be, the moral and strategic questions of how a nation can and should respond to such massive
violence as that which was hurled against the United States
on September 11, 2001. This is, to me, basically a question
about how a nation such as the United States, or any nation,
can struggle toward generating dynamics of mutuality, rather
than domination and control, in a global context in which the
latter dynamics are pervasive and predictable.

To generate dynamics of mutuality is not the easy way for
us to go, but it is the hope of the world. It requires creativity and courage and most of all, from the United States,
humility. Its seeds have been planted historically by movements of nonviolent resistance and are being planted today
through peace-building efforts; commitments to restorative justice; and theologies of liberation, feminism, womanism, and
other movements of justice-making with compassion — movements of people who know that any lasting efforts at building
justice and peace must be multilateral, cross-cultural, interreligious, and international in scope. They must also be rooted
and grounded in careful attentiveness to the well-being of creation and creatures that are other-than-human. Otherwise, our
human efforts for justice and compassion will always fall short.

One of the most predictable and discouraging aspects of the
crisis fomented by these attacks has been the relatively uncreative and unbalanced U.S. response in which there have been
few public places in the political arena for serious discussions
about how the United States might seek to build a more deeply
mutual relation with other nations, friends or foe.

Our reaction was uncreative because, without a carefully
constructed and sustainable global coalition and international
plan, the U.S. military rhetoric and campaign (waged in con-
cert basically with only a few allies) is likely to destroy more

than it can create in the Middle East, back home in the United States, and elsewhere. Our patriotic displays of flags, fundraising, and fanfare notwithstanding, a great deal is being lost here at home, beginning with some of our basic liberties and, as importantly, our collective sense of hospitality to the stranger and the "other." Even before September 11, the latter was not one of our strongest features as a nation, but it was at least a value to which most United States citizens aspired.

Our military assault on Afghanistan (and whomever may be next) and the stripping of basic human rights from those whom we fear in the U.S. and elsewhere has also been a spiritually unbalanced response. With little or no attention paid by the leaders of our nation to the many thoughtful, seasoned advocates of *satyagraha* and nonviolent resistance throughout the world, the Bush administration has emerged as a big-time war machine. And the military effort is being supported, though not without dissent, by at least the major patriarchal, monotheistic religious organizations in the nation — Christian, Jewish, and Muslim. There seems to be little space in the national conversation for serious public debate about nonviolent options, about what the U.S. might do next besides make more war or, among Christians, about where the Spirit of *ahimsa* — she who is our *satyagraha* — may be dwelling these days.

This means that the United States of America is way off balance. We are in danger not only of devastating others but also of being badly damaged ourselves, collectively and individually. In the midst of all the patriotism, it's hard to notice that the nation is in harm's way not simply from terrorists but, on a daily and pervasive basis, from ourselves. Out of balance, our national "soul" is being shaped by the press, which long ago became the servant of our government, and by our civil religion, which can be summed up in the "God Bless America" rhetoric that decks the highways and byways, restaurants and retail stores of this nation. In this stressful context, we the people of the United States seem to have lost our capacity for measured judgment as well as compassion for those who are not "like us."

Now obviously a strong response was called for by the
United States, perhaps even the military elimination of the
Taliban, something that could and should have happened years
ago, given the brutalizing of women about which the Taliban
made no secret and seemed almost proud. I am among a large
minority of U.S. citizens who, from day one, has been advo-
cating the building up of an *international* coalition, under the
auspices of the United Nations, to fight terrorism primarily
through struggling for justice and peace and not through war.
For I believe that the only way to win the fight against powers
of domination — including terrorism — is to struggle mutually,
with other nations and across cultures, toward building soci-
eties in which sharing resources on the basis of ability and need
provides a moral foundation for us all. This should become a
social, economic, and political goal for all nations and cultures.

There will always, of course, be "strongmen" and "warlords"
like bin Laden whose lust for power and dominion threatens
the peace of the world. And there will always be men and
women vulnerable to being manipulated by these charismatic
zealots for domination and violent control. Terrorism is not
a new thing, and it's not something that will be eliminated
by war.

The only way to win the current war against terrorism is for
the United States, in the context of a global network, to join
in helping create justice and compassion throughout the Arab
world. This would include the creation of a Palestinian state
alongside a peaceful Israel, an effort that the United States —
in its passive acceptance of Prime Minister Ariel Sharon's
renowned hostility toward Palestine — seems determined to
undermine. To help create justice and compassion in the Arab
world and elsewhere, the United States would also need to be
breaking our economic dependence on the repressive ruling
oligarchies of oil-rich nations like Saudi Arabia. This in turn
would require our joining other nations and peoples in building up alternative sources of energy that would exploit neither
humans nor other creatures and natural resources.

The fact that the Bush administration shows no interest in these goals does not mean that they are not worth pursuing. It means that other nations will need to persuade the United States to cooperate in building a global movement for peace. If the U.S. refuses to be moved in this direction, other nations will need to find ways to strategically educate and isolate the United States in international efforts to build peace with justice. If effective, this strategy would leave us to fight terrorism by ourselves, which might shake our national leaders into joining, rather than continuing to resist, serious international efforts at peace-building. The alternatives to the United States learning how to cooperate with other nations in today's world are very grim indeed.

After all, we may dispatch bin Laden and his closest comrades, as we seem to have already ousted the Taliban, at least officially, at the time of this writing. But we will be fooling ourselves if we imagine that we are therefore winning the war against terrorism. For every Osama who is killed or disappears, a thousand more young men (and women?) will rise up to carry on where he and his fallen comrades have left off. What we in the United States call "terrorism" will only multiply and thrive.

But the people of the United States with folks elsewhere around the world can, together, find ways to respond creatively to those princes of violence and destruction who enjoy watching passenger jets explode into buildings filled with people. Clearly, the war against terrorism must be waged primarily as a struggle for economic and social justice — a struggle for radical mutuality — throughout the Arab world and wherever else in the world desperate people are taking up arms against those who are, or who represent to them, their oppressors.

So the war against terrorism, if it is to be won, must be basically a struggle for right relation, justice, or mutuality between and among us all, here in the United States and elsewhere. In this larger context, the military campaign being waged against the Al Qaeda terrorist network, whatever we may think of it, however much we may support or oppose it, can be only one dimension of a much longer, more complex struggle. We must see that it is not a war that we or anyone (including terrorists) can win with weapons. The United States is as mistaken as Al Qaeda about the long-term effectiveness of using violence to conquer enemies.

Liberating Faith vs. Religions of Desperation

The second way in which the terrorist attacks sharpened for me the issue of mutuality that reaches far beyond humankind toward all species and creatures was by sparking a spiritual and moral question of whether God is not only a creative Spirit of mutuality, but also—*within* the struggle for mutuality—a destructive force. Let me explain.

In one of my earlier books, I wrestled with the question of "human agency"—that is, *our power as humans* to help build a more just and loving world.[13] I had a wonderful time writing that book! It began as my doctoral dissertation in the late 1970s at Union Theological Seminary in New York. It was a joy and a privilege to be working with my advisors and my sister and brother students who were filled with similar longings for justice and peace and with many of the same moral questions about how we humans might help create such a world. In that dissertation, published several years later as *The Redemption of God: A Theology of Mutual Relation,* I wrote that we humans are indeed responsible, in and through the power of God, for taking care of the world, for making justice and building peace. I believed then and perhaps, if possible, even more now that God is our power in mutual relation; that whenever we are struggling for mutual or right relation we are "godding"; and that God's own life in the world is interdependent with ours. In other words, we are in mutual relation with God as well as with one another. We are created to be God's friends and lovers.

At the time, I did not pay much attention to the rest of

the created world, to the creatures that are other than human. Looking back, I see this as a serious omission rooted in the failure of modern human cultures and certainly monotheistic (and other) religions in most parts of the world to treat creation and other-than-human creatures with the sort of deep respect and carefulness we tend to reserve for that which we experience as sacred, such as (sometimes, somewhat more commonly) the sanctity of our sister and brother humans.

Why is it so hard for us to get clear about the sacredness of other creatures? One reason, I believe, is that our human species seems almost resigned to the inevitability of violence against one another — humans and others. Moreover, Christians, Jews, and Muslims alike are used to assuming that violence can be, and often is, the work of God.

Consider what happened on September 11, 2001. What probably was most shocking for many of us about those attacks was that this mission of devastation and death was undertaken in the name of God by young men who genuinely believed they were acting on behalf of a God whom they, no less than most Christians, believed to be a God of Love.

But does a God of Love destroy us in order to save us or others? Does He, or She, or such a Sacred One love creation by wiping out thousands of people who are going about their daily lives? No.

Does such a God do such a thing for any good reason? No.

Did the God of Israel actually obliterate the Canaanites in times past, as the Hebrew Bible suggests? No.

Does this same God terrorize Palestinian or Israeli civilians today? No.

Does God bomb abortion clinics and murder abortion providers? No.

But there are also questions that are harder for some of us to answer: Does God ever willfully destroy some human or other creature? Does God execute prisoners? Does God perform abortions? Does God wear fur? Does God eat meat? Why are these questions harder for some of us to answer definitively? Because we are aware of moral complexities that inhere in these situations, quandaries and questions that seem to us not as present in the decision to fly a passenger plane into a building filled with people. Not that the attackers on September 11 were not morally complex men; I have no idea what their lives and decision processes were like. But the murder of thousands of people was justified on the basis of a very absolutist theology that does not allow for complexity, ambiguity, or balance. This same kind of absolutist, unbalanced thinking has undergirded the activities of Operation Rescue and other terrorist organizations and individuals who have assaulted abortion providers in the U.S.

Absolutist theologies make no space for moral ambiguity and debate. They discourage honest wrestling with questions of right and wrong. As such, they tend to squeeze God — a Spirit of honest struggle — out of the picture. On issues of capital punishment, abortion, and the slaughter of animals for food and fur, there usually is at least some space for disagreement and debate, even among many of the proponents of these practices, as to where lines get drawn between when the practice is right and when it's wrong. This is why it's harder to say, in the abstract, whether abortion or capital punishment or the raising of livestock for slaughter and food is right or wrong. For many of us, the most honest moral response is "It depends."

It depends on many variables in real-life situations. Yet the margin for error in capital punishment is virtually nonexistent, and its effects are so devastating to so many (not just the condemned), that I am strongly opposed to it in all cases, even those in which a good moral case could be made for it — such as with Timothy McVeigh and, probably, Osama bin Laden.

Like capital punishment and the slaughter of people in war, the slaughter of animals is, to me, a morally shameful economic enterprise upon which most of humankind has learned to depend, directly or indirectly. For personal nutrition as well as for larger social reasons, I am trying to incorporate an increasingly vegan way of eating into my life, which is no easy thing. I share the class privilege that undergirds most vegan and vegetarian efforts in the U.S. today. It takes money to buy fresh vegetables and meat-substitutes, to try to eat ethically! Still, I want to support national and global efforts to create more sustainable and humane alternatives to raising and eating livestock.

As for abortion, I will always hold sacred the belief that every woman should be able to choose whether or not to bear children and should have the social right and medical options to choose an abortion if she must. I also believe that the larger society, including religious organizations, should help provide moral markers for drawing lines between any woman's "right to choose" and the "viability" of her fetus. In the United States, these "markers" were established in *Roe v. Wade* (1973), a decision I respect and celebrate.

God in Relation to Death, Destruction, and Evil

But the question still remains: Does God destroy life as well as create it? Is God ever the executioner? We have already looked at the image of God as Warrior, with implications that God is sometimes, perhaps more often than we can bear to imagine, involved in killing. But how do we know if and when God is involved in actions that take lives of humans or other creatures? When is the creator God also the Spirit of destruction and death? Most Christians probably assume that God is involved, at the very least through noninterference, in all death and destruction. Certainly in relation to creatures that are not human, most Christians take for granted that God is involved in the slaughter of animals and in the depletion of air, soil, and water, as long as this devastation is on behalf of human well-being.

On the other hand, the possibility of God's involvement in death-bearing activities raises hard questions for many Christians, perhaps harder for many Christians than for some other religious practitioners, because Christian spirituality tends to be so idealistic. If something is tough, that is, we tend to spiritualize it, which can make it easier for us to deal with. A little boy is killed in an accident. Some Christians will say things like, "God called him home," or "God must have had a reason." After the terrorist attacks, Christian leaders Jerry Falwell and Pat Robertson were among many Christian conservatives who looked for the reason God had allowed such a thing to happen — and found it in their perceptions of other peoples' sins.

The need to understand what God is doing, and why, often runs deep in religious consciousness, not only among Christians. People of faith naturally want to know where we stand in relation to God, and major crises tend to sharpen our need to know. This was Job's predicament, and it is one that most religious people share to varying degrees at different times throughout our lives. There are so many events in our life together — like the deaths of people by violence or, for that matter, from cancer — that we seldom can fully understand. In response to such losses, and often in grief, when we cannot find scientific or other earthbound reasons that satisfy us, many of us turn to God. Either we blame God: a neighbor said to me the other day, "At the death of my son, I lost my faith." Or we put our trust, a deeply sad trust, in God: our trust that he knows what he's doing, or that she must have a reason. This last response to death and destruction, which was Job's, is probably the most common among Christians: God has a reason, a plan, that we humans don't know; and destruction and death are part of God's plan. In other words, for most Christians — Jews and Muslims too — God is not only a creator; he is also a destroyer. (I intentionally am using the masculine pronoun in this discussion).

But we monotheists are far too inclined to "personalize" God as both creator and destroyer and to assume that he acts like we do, except on a much larger scale. In truth, we wind up creating "God" in our image and then justifying our behavior by insisting that we are doing "God's will" — whether it is bombing terrorists or ministering to the sick and the homeless. A more honest spiritual reckoning is possible, I believe, when we realize that God really is not a person like us. God is not a person, period. God is a spiritual presence that we, like Jesus, can experience in deeply personal ways. But God really is not simply a larger, better version of a human being. God is more like the air we breathe and the ground we walk on. To be sure, the Spirit that is God takes human shape through our lives — and creature shape through the lives of all living beings. But that does not mean that God can be pinned down as "more" in Jesus than in the Buddha, or more in Gautama than in Mohammed, or more in Mohammed than in Mary, Jesus' mother, or Peter, Jesus' friend, or you or me, or the sea bass or the locust tree.

Jesus and other prophets and saints of God may indeed have embodied and, as such, loved God in very special ways. Indeed, we Christians believe that something of this sort happened in Jesus' life. We believe that Jesus was rooted and grounded in God in amazing ways. But this does not mean that God loved Jesus more than us; or that God loves any person more than others or that God loves people more than birds and fish and cattle. The Spirit of God does not discriminate in this way by choosing some creatures to love more and others less.

We humans (and others too?) decide how deeply in God, the Holy Spirit of mutuality, we will ground our lives. This decision takes the shape of a faith rooted often in leaps of imagination and consciousness rather than in any rational knowledge. And this faith is what matters. It makes all the difference in the world — to God and the world, to humans and other creatures.

Theodicy, or the theological question of how God is related to evil, is not so much a problem for nonmonotheists. This is because if we know we are *in* God, we know that our dying as well as our living is in God. We are never outside of God or without God. But can we who make war then claim, with our terrorist enemy, that our killing is also in God and, in some sense, part of "God's will"?

I believe that the answer to this critical moral question is both yes and no. Remember Gandhi. If our motive genuinely is love — the building of right relation, justice with compassion, mutuality that requires that we respect our enemies as well as our own friends and kin — then the war we make may be waged as part of God's own movement. *But not necessarily.* Because motive is never enough. We must do more than intend to build a just world and hope that it is compassionate as well. We must learn how to genuinely love our enemies as ourselves. A genuine love of our enemy requires us to do everything in our power not to harm or humiliate the enemy. If we are doing everything we can to respect and value our enemy as we would like to be respected and valued ourselves, then we truly are doing everything we can to embody God's Spirit and, in that sense, God's will. In such a case, we can well imagine — in humility, not triumph — that our war, including the killing that we do, sadly reflects at least shadows and intimations of God's will.

With this enemy-love, our killing is always sad. It may wind up being tragic. We may learn that it was necessary — or, perhaps, unnecessary. But our killing will never be simply good or right, and if we love our enemies, we will always be well aware of this. *Without* enemy-love, any killing that we do is not merely sad or unfortunate, not just "collateral damage" or the "unavoidable" effects of war. To kill without loving our enemy is evil. It is also "in God," as is everything. But such loveless killing is not good. It is wrong, it is immoral, and we should not be doing it — not in this war, not in any war.

Most war that we make, including the war against terrorism, is evil because it has little enemy-love except from time to time on the parts of individual soldiers whose compassion and capacity for enemy-love have made them "good warriors."

Terrorism is evil because it has no place for enemy-love. Without enemy-love — which means respecting the basic rights and dignity even of those whom we hate — there is nothing about violence that can be truly liberating and nothing about war, "theirs" or "ours," that is even remotely holy.

For many Christians, it is at least thinkable to struggle with theological and ethical nuances about the sadness, and often the evil, of killing human enemies. It is much more difficult for most Christians to even imagine sustaining serious reflection on the ethics of killing other creatures and destroying the creation. The spiritual trivialization of creatures and creation is steeped in the long-standing Christian assumption that only humans have souls — that is, intrinsic spiritual value, a "meeting place" with the divine, a dimension of creaturely being that seeks and can receive salvation. This arrogant anthropocentrism — human-centeredness — sits close to the core of all patriarchal religion, not only Christianity. It is rooted in scientific and spiritual ignorance, and it reflects an out-of-touchness with our own most soulful possibilities. Split off from right-relation with the rest of creation, we humans are unable to make right-relation with one another or with God. We humans are in need of help. To whom can we turn? Why not other animals and the rest of creation?

God in All Creation

One thing about the other animals: they teach us not to idealize life and death, violence and peace, and the Spirit in which it all happens. Like humans, most animals kill. They kill to protect themselves. They kill to eat. They kill because they want more of a good thing, such as land, food, or sex. It is not true that we humans are the only species that kills without good reason. So it would be unwise to adopt the rest of creation as a teacher of relational ethics and it is nonsense to look to nature to teach us much about nonviolent resistance, for the rest of creation evidently is as fiercely violent as we humans are.

So to look to the animals and the earth for help in making right, mutual relation is not a matter of turning to moral superiors or even to innocent beings. We should turn to the earth and its creatures not because they are "better" than we are, but because they are our sisters and brothers. They, no less than we, reflect God's image. They, no less than we, have "souls," places in which they, in their particular identity, and God, in her universal Spirit, touch and are mutually transformed. We look to the animals and the earth not because they need us, because we need them as much as they do us and, in many cases, we need them much more than they need us. We turn to the animals and the earth because, with them, we can probe new dimensions of mutuality and God and come to life in startling ways. We get to know these other creatures, and we see that all creatures, human and other, are much more alike than different in both spiritual and scientific ways.

In the realm of violence, however, there is one significant difference between humans and the rest of creation. The violence done by humans is often not merely to destroy but to humiliate and increase suffering. Such violence is more than cruel. It is sadistic — suffering and cruelty imposed at least partially for the pleasure of the torturer.

How is this different from a cat's torturing a mouse? I think it's fair to suggest that the cat probably doesn't enjoy the mouse's suffering but rather the pleasure of the sport of doing battle with a living — squirming, squealing — opponent. Sadism is the emotional enjoyment of another's suffering and is probably unique to the human species. It is a perversion or distortion of God's image, in which the human sadist enjoys the painful effects of dominating some person or creature. If God is our power in mutual relation, we can surely say that the enjoyment of domination is not an aspect of the divine image. To be in God's image in this world involves struggling to transform, not to take pleasure in, systems of violent domination and dynamics of coercion.

As sadistic as human beings so often are toward one another, the cruelty we continue to inflict on the rest of the created world — animals and natural resources — is beyond our capacity to imagine. This is because most of us regard animals, earth, and water as possessions and ourselves as their owners. We assume it is our God-given right to do with them as we please. More often than we like to realize, human beings take a great deal of pleasure in hurting and destroying our brother and sister creatures.

Terrorizing Creation

We chase the animals. We trap them. We terrify them. We enjoy the hunt. We set them up. We shoot them. We cook them and eat them. We enjoy our food.

We raise them in small crates. We do not allow them to move. We look at them and see "things," not living creatures. We deny that there's any moral issue here. We pump their bodies full of chemicals to make them attractive to the human eye. We frighten them. We buy and sell them. We cook and eat them. We enjoy our meals.

We raise them. We tie them up. We brand them. We beat them, if we must. We chain them. We agitate them. We sell them and eat them. We enjoy them.

We breed them to race. We train them to run faster and faster. We do whatever we must — whip them, drug them, starve them — to make them winners. We enjoy a good race, especially a winner.

We breed them to fight. We kick them and beat them. We chain them and starve them to make them mean. We like watching them fight to the death. We enjoy their sport, especially the killers.

We devastate the forests. We poison the waters. We chase the animals away from their habitats. We run over them on the roads. We leave them dead or dying. We are sorry about the animals, but we enjoy our new homes and our good roads.

We deplete the earth's soil. We desecrate the earth's land. We rip down the earth's trees, strip her mountains, pollute her waters, foul her air, torture her body — and we dare to call other people "terrorists."

"*Elephant God, Forgive Us*"

Human beings should bow down before the One who meets us through the other creatures and make our confession:

We have sinned against Thee in thought, word, and deed, by what we have done and by what we have left undone. We have not loved the other creatures as we do ourselves — and we do not love ourselves all that well. We have not loved the Holy Spirit that actually meets us in the chickens and the cows that we eat, the horses and the dogs that we tame, the wolves and the sea turtles whose habitats we have claimed for ourselves. We have regarded animals and earth primarily as resources for our human food, our human sport, our human pleasure. We have not loved the animals, the earth and water and air, as our sisters and brothers. We have not seen clearly that God lives in each blade of grass, each grain of sand, each snail and ant.

We do not yet know how to live on this planet without killing other humans in order to protect ourselves from violence and harm — look at this war against terrorism and our ghastly system of criminal *injustice,* including capital punishment. We also do not know how to live on the earth without destroying other creatures for our own use — to eat them, to enjoy them, or to stay safe from whatever disease, discomfort, or danger they may bring.

It may be that the human species is not far enough evolved to know how to live safely and peaceably on the planet with all of creation, human and other. Or such a notion may reflect an outmoded optimism about where we humans are headed and what we humans can become. But I hope not.[14]

I pray the day will come on earth when Christians and people of other spiritual traditions will know that what Christians have called the Incarnation was not simply the coming of the Holy One in the life, death, and resurrection of one human creature, Jesus, and the religious tradition generated in his memory.

We will know on that day that God is, and always has been,

really present through the whole created universe, including this planet and its many varied species, including humans. We will see that, just as God has many human faces, and not just one, so too does she have the faces and bodies of many creatures, not just humans. We will realize that we humans and other creatures "god" together.

In the meantime, it is up to us here on earth to help find and keep a balance between an ever deepening respect for human beings, ourselves and others, and what is for many of us a more recently cultivated respect for other creatures as they are in themselves, not simply as we can use them for food and pleasure.

There's no question in my mind that, for reasons of both morality and health, we should eat less meat, and probably none. Most of us, certainly those of us who live in warmer climates, should not wear skins or furs of animals that have been killed for these "products." Because this view is not yet shared by most Christians or others in the United States or elsewhere, we have to really struggle with these ethical issues in order to keep our balance. Our churches should be helping cultivate this ethical awareness and empowering us, in the name of God, to wrestle with such questions. For we Christians should be pioneers in the journey toward that realm in which the lion, lamb, and human child can lie down together in peace.

> Elephant God forgive us.
> Holy mountain shelter us.
> Sister spirit stream carry us on.
> Tiny sparrow sing to us
>   your favorite hymn.
> Pelican brother Jesus,
>   cover us with your wings.
> Bid us goodnight
>   and raise us in the morning
>   in your christic power
>   to recreate the world.

The Horse as Priest

Once I had decided to initiate a therapeutic riding program, I began talking with everyone I could about how to do it. In May 2000, shortly after meeting Barbara Doughty, executive director of "Flying Changes" Center for Therapeutic Riding in Topsham, Maine, I had breakfast with Larnie Otis, a former student at Episcopal Divinity School who is currently a priest in Maine. As we were catching up, I mentioned to her my emerging interest in therapeutic riding. Larnie put down her fork, shook her head in astonishment, and spoke with excitement. She said that, prior to seminary, she herself had been deeply involved in therapeutic horseback riding. "If you go in this direction, Carter," she said, "you'll discover that the horse is the priest." More than a year later and still early in the operations of "Free Rein," our therapeutic horseback riding center in North Carolina, I am just beginning to understand: *the horse is the priest.*

A Traditional Interpretation: Priest Mediates God's Power

First of all, even from a rather traditional Christian perspective, to assert that the horse is priest is not simply to lift up a poetic image, nor is it hyperbole. It is theology, good theology, the kind rooted in a living spirituality. If God is the creative wellspring of all that lives and breathes and loves, and

---

This chapter was written in late August 2001 for publication in an issue of *The Witness* that was postponed due to the terrorist attacks.

if God meets us through those who offer us occasions to drink from this healing spring, then surely it is this same Holy Spirit that a horse offers to the child or adult who comes, seeking strength. The priest in the Catholic tradition is, after all, fashioned theologically as a mediator, one who stands at the altar for both God and humanity, in some way representing each to the other. This is what the horse is doing at the altar of the therapeutic arena — bringing together the human rider and her or his restorative, healing power. The horse is helping open the rider to this sacred energy and, we can faithfully imagine, helping open God to the embodied yearnings and needs of a particular human (and horse).

From this very Catholic perspective, therapeutic horseback riding, like the Eucharist, can be an occasion of thanksgiving, in which creatures and our divine life are united through our mutual participation in the holiest of sacrifices — God's giving up of divine control in order to be there with, and for, those in need. Giving its body over to the person's need for strength and health, the horse represents God in this transaction. The horse also represents our creaturely moral capacity to give ourselves over to empowering one another and other creatures to go together (walking, trotting, cantering, if you will) in right, more fully mutual, relationship, in which we move together, more nearly as one, creatures united.

At the same time, the human rider, empowered through the horse — like all who share in the holy Eucharist — represents all humans and other creatures who need to draw our strength, our sacred power, from struggling for right, justice-making, compassionate connectedness with one another. This right relation is forged through our willingness, following Jesus, to give up our spiritually ignorant claims to autonomy and independence in order to be there for one another in an authentically holy communion. The building of such community — like the creative relational connectedness between horse and rider and those who accompany them — always generates sacred space in which miracles can happen.

Beyond Catholicism: Priestly Riders

That's a fairly traditional Christian interpretation of the horse's role as priest. But it pushes well beyond Catholic interpretation in one way and Protestant in another. And both of these movements beyond much of our theological heritage are significant. The images offered here move beyond Catholicism in the assumption that the human rider as well as the horse can be priest. The autistic child, the teenager at risk, the addicted woman or man not only represents our human/creaturely need for one another's presence and solidarity. These priestly riders, male and female, young and old, also offer us experiences and images of the sacred power that touch and change not only human life but the rest of creation as well.

At its best, therapeutic horseback riding is a mutual endeavor, in which the horse, as well as the rider, is affected — touched, empowered, often brought to new life. For many feminist Christians, this radical mutuality rings deeply true in the Jesus story as well, in which the brother from Nazareth is not the only agent of sacred, healing power. Rather, like the horse, Jesus receives healing energy even as he gives it. Indeed, his sacred power is "sacred" precisely because it is shared — a powerfully Holy Spirit because it belongs to no one, but rather to all.

In the Jesus story, in the Christian Eucharist, and in therapeutic riding, God is not simply represented by Jesus, the ordained priest, or the horse. God is the power, the sacred healing energy, that is generated between and among all the characters in the drama — Jesus and the rest of people, the priest and the rest of the people, the horse and the rider and the rest of the creatures, human and others, with them. Larnie Otis was right. The horse is the priest — and so is the person with special needs who comes seeking healing and strength.

Beyond Protestantism: Sacred Creation

The implication of this theology that spins us way beyond Protestantism is its profound affirmation of creatures-other-than-human as being as much in God, of God, and part of God's healing, liberating work as we humans can be. Is it a sacrilege or a sacramental revelation to affirm that the horse, like Jesus, is our priest? Does it move us outside the bounds of Christian faith, or can it deepen and radicalize our Christian witness, to claim that therapeutic horseback riding is as filled with the presence and power of the living God as any place of Christian worship can be?

As a priest, I have no doubt that Christian worship and sacrament has for too long been not only patronizingly male-centered but also arrogantly human-centered. We have been unfaithful to the rest of God's creation, and thus to God. Realizing this in my soul, I am grateful to be able to turn to the horse and rider as my own priest. I am filled with awe in my yearning to be open to whatever God may be teaching us in new ways. Or is it that we are being called to something God has been teaching since before the worlds began — an ancient wisdom, a dimension of Sophia, which some of us late learners may be hearing and seeing for the first time? In the context of therapeutic riding, is my vocation now to become an acolyte to horse and rider?

An Almost Unbearable Lightness of Being

In Celebration of Sister Angela

Wendy Hope Solling (known as "Sister Angela," a member of the Anglican Community of Clare) died on January 20, 2002. Angela had been living for the past two years with us at Redbud Springs, an intentional community near Brevard, North Carolina, where she and I were working together on a number of projects, including helping develop Free Rein Center for Therapeutic Riding and Education. Angela was a primary inspiration for this book. Here is what I said at her funeral.

What did you most treasure about Angela? Was it her way of greeting every living soul — "Hello, daahling!"? Was it her use of words like "dancey" and "gorgeous" to describe every glorious waking moment with every person and creature she ever met? Was it her energy, enthusiasm, and excitement about being alive in the Light, which she believed to the core of her being was the essence of God and of all that matters in this and every world? Or was it the plain and simple fact that, when you were with her, you felt so loved, affirmed, and good about yourself?

I met Angela in January 1991, eleven years ago, when I was a guest at the monastery in Stroud, New South Wales, which is several hours northwest of Sydney, Australia. As many of you know, Angela and several other nuns and helpers had built the

---

This sermon was preached at St. Phillip's Episcopal Church, Brevard, North Carolina, on February 9, 2002, and again at the Episcopal Church of the Good Shepherd, Watertown, Massachusetts, on March 5, 2002, in celebration of Sister Angela.

monastery at Stroud with their own hands. The sisters and their friends had done this with mud bricks, which they themselves made out of Australian clay. "Sister Angela," as she was known in England and Australia, oversaw this construction project some twenty-five years ago, immediately after she had been diagnosed with colon cancer and given two months to live, or two years at the outside. "No, daahling," she told her doctor, "it's not my time. I have a monastery to build." And so she did.

Some of you may not realize that Wendy Hope Solling (later, Sister Angela) was one of Australia's premier young sculptors in the late 1940s and 1950s, working in wire and metal on themes related to the Australian outback. Later, when she entered the Anglican Community of St. Clare at Freeland in England, she began working in wood, stone, and metal to make religious sculptures, which today are treasures in various churches, monasteries, and cathedrals in England and Australia. Just last week, a member of one of the Franciscan communities told me that she recently had had the "privilege" of cleaning several of Sister Angela's sculptures in England, and that a startling light comes through, or emanates from, each of these pieces, giving each sculpture a special sense of lightness and grace.

The thing about Angela that I was, and am, most touched and transformed by was, and is, the lightness of her being, a quality of body and soul, of intuition and insight, of artistic genius and athletic grace, that had, and has, nothing to do with size and everything to do with a quality of relational presence that we often call "love."

As you can tell, it is difficult to speak of Angela in the past tense, not because I am in denial about her death, but because Angela herself would be the first to insist that far from being gone from us, those who have died have simply moved on into another dimension of life in the Spirit and are, in some ways, even more present to us now than when they were living persons here on earth. So please bear with me as I fumble around among verb tenses in reflecting on the spiritual legacy of Wendy Hope Solling, whom we knew as Sister Angela, or simply as Angela.

Wisdom 7:22–30 reminds those of us steeped in patriarchal Christianity that Wisdom, or Sophia, is an eternal image of Sacred Power. Indeed, just as Jesus is for Christians the Word of God and the Christ of God, so too is Jesus the Sophia or Wisdom of God. She was with God in the beginning. All that came to be had life in her, and that life was the Light of humankind and creaturekind, a Light that shines in the darkness, a light that darkness cannot overcome. The passage from Wisdom was read here to remind us that Sister Angela was a feminist Christian, a woman who refused to forget her sisters or to ignore their struggles for justice, struggles that over time she recognized as her own.

It is imperative that we today not bury our female saints, priests, and prophets without recognizing how trivialized or dismissed most of them were, and are to this day. Angela's femaleness was not an insignificant dimension of who she was. It mattered to her. It mattered to her because it gave her particular perspectives, as both artist and religious leader, in a world and church dominated by men. Again and again, like many women religious and women priests, the Rev. Sister Angela's mystical spirituality was dismissed by the powers that be as flaky. All the while, her talent — to be honest, her genius — as a world-class sculptor was much admired throughout her life and sometimes sought after by church leaders who winked and smiled at her spirituality. It never seemed to dawn on these serious custodians of the faith that the light that shines through her sculpture is the same God that shone through her embodied person here on this earth!

But being a woman mattered most to Sister Angela because her womanness was a place of relational connection with women of all ages and conditions who frequented the monastery and sought her out for counsel. Later in her life, Angela's spirituality and wisdom, seasoned through her experience as the leader of the Clare Community in Australia, provided a path to

Aboriginal women whose own leaders teamed up with Angela to share sources of spiritual strength, hope, and experience.

Before meeting Angela, I had seen a film called *The Fully Ordained Meat Pie,* a reference to a quip made by a priest in the Anglican Church of Australia that ordaining a woman would be like consecrating a meat pie! In case you don't get it — and many sane and intelligent people don't — many guardians of patriarchal religion have argued over time that it is impossible for God to ordain women, because like meat pies, we lack something that God needs his priests to have. Your guess is as good as mine as to what it is we may lack! Be that as it may, the great film on the meat pie showed Sister Angela consoling a group of Australian women in the aftermath of yet another defeat for the ordination of women in 1987. She spoke with such passion to the grieving and angry women gathered in the monastery, "Now, daahlings, you must not let them get you down. You must laugh in the face of the tiger! That's what you must do — *laugh,* daahlings, in the face of the tiger!"

I'll never forget watching that film and asking the people I was with, "Who *is* that woman, that wonderful nun?" For Angela was — is — like Jesus. And that was, and is, the point.

For those of us who would at times find ourselves befuddled and frustrated by the possibility that Angela never had a linear thought in her life, try to imagine what it must have been like hanging out with Jesus of Nazareth in his more mystical moments! Angela knew that she wasn't always the easiest person to work with, but this was of little bother to her unless she felt that either she or others were lacking compassion or generosity of spirit. She didn't often get angry, but when she did, watch out! Usually in response to an experience or report of some cruelty or injustice, she would let it rip! This was no sugar-coated sister.

The Gospel of John was Angela's favorite book in the Bible, and of course. Because the author of John believes that God is not only with us; God lives through us! Indeed, for John and Angela, the good news is not merely that God is our Father or Mother or that Jesus is our Savior. For Christians, this is good news, but the best news, for Christians and everyone, is that we ourselves are God-bearers, put here in life to bear love and justice to the world! And not just those of us who are Christians, but all people. And not just we humans, but all creatures, from the great trees to the horses that Angela cherished to each wave of the sea and grain of sand, each twig and turtle! All of us are God-bearers. Each person, each creature, each in our own beautiful way. That was the heart of Angela's faith and it is, I believe, what drew us to her — and her to us.

For Angela, like the author of John, Christian life was not primarily about religion or theology, not mainly about religious worship or about waiting to be more fully in the Light of God some day. For Angela, like the author of the Gospel of John, life each day was participation in the living God of Light and Love. Her whole reason for being was to let God's Light shine through her — which brings me to her "angelic" lightness of being. Was it not because the Light of God shone through her right into our lives that we felt so affirmed and good when she was with us?

Is this not what all angels do? Illuminate our lives, shine sacred light upon us, help us see ourselves as we are meant to be. My mother has a poem and colorful graphic on her bathroom wall that reads, "Most people don't know that there are angels whose only job is to make sure you don't get too comfortable and fall asleep and miss your life."

"Come on, Carter, you don't believe in angels, do you?" Some of you are probably whispering to yourselves! Well yes, actually, I do. Not the Hallmark Card variety, but something much more like our Angela. Not only human angels and not simply individuals, but divine beings beyond our capacities to imagine — mighty spiritual forces that come to us through people and water and rocks and birds and beasts and the power of collective memories and stories, forces with the power and energy of God, connecting us generation to generation, moving our struggles, touching our hearts, opening our minds, transforming our lives, and seasoning our capacities to bear the Sacred Spirit with and for one another so that we do not miss our lives.

Dear sisters and brothers, Wendy Hope Solling, our friend Angela, was and is an angel. But lest we give her too much spiritual authority and ourselves too little, let's look a little deeper still at what is going on here. Through Angela's spirit now so fully mingled with and in God, some interesting things have been happening in my waking and sleeping since Angela's death on January 20, each of them shaking me up so that I will not miss my life. With the passing of each day, the force of this beloved sister's love has become clearer and ever more compelling, and her word to me, and to you, is this: "Dearheart, the point is not that *I* am in the Light. Of course I am. But the point is that *you* are in the Light! We are all here together in the Light of God — but isn't it just *glorious!*"

It's what she was all about, and what she still is all about — to help us see that it's what *we're* all here to do: to live fully in the Light of God, to let the light shine through us, to share a way of being that is so light and so loving and so good humored and, yes, sometimes so angry at cruelty and injustice as to be almost unbearable.

It is a vocation we share: to be God-bearers, to share sacred power, to take flight with Angela through all eternity, beginning here and now wherever we are. We are called through Angela's spirit, wherever we are, to live with eyes open to the world and God, and to let ourselves — our minds and spirits — expand. We are invited by Angela, whoever we are, to grow spiritually larger, a day at a time and, as we grow, not to give much of a whit about others' opinions of us. The vocation we share with our beloved sister is to foster loving, mutual relationships and to do whatever we can to help build a just and compassionate world and communities in which all humans and creatures are respected.

Angels, of course, see through the eyes of God. As we

learn to see more clearly through the eyes of God, we will be learning how better to love ourselves, the world, and God. Like Angela, and like Jesus, we too will care less about rules than about love, justice, and compassion. And we will care much less about strange human fixations like an overly zealous patriotism and overly structured religion than about doing whatever we can on behalf of the well-being of the entire created order — across lines of race, culture, religion, class, nation, gender, sexual identity, and even species.

But let's not think that it's all seriousness and struggle! Angels have fun and great senses of humor! In Angela's spirit, we are free to play and laugh and enjoy these lives of ours! She, for example, was working on perfecting her cantering with Red, the quarter horse whom she and I shared. And she would have loved the Super Bowl this year, especially its patriotic outcome, and she was so looking forward to going to Red Sox games (she called them "Red Stockings").

I will always remember one of the last moments she and I spent together, the day before her stroke. Angela and I were in the car, headed down the mountain for church, where we had become much involved in helping put together a new, more inclusive liturgy on Sunday afternoons. We were both a bit stressed about the controversy spinning around about the service. But Angela and I had our own little ways of handling stress when things got to us. So, mimicking Red the horse — who is a "cribber," which means that when she's stressed, she chews on wood for the purpose of windsucking, kind of like a child sucking her thumb — I glanced over at Angela and went [I imitated Red cribbing]. Angela instantly went right back at me [Angela imitated Red cribbing] and we said together, "Oh, daahling!" We burst out laughing and the tension floated lightly away.

Two days later, the day after her stroke, I left the hospital and drove home to take a bath and do some chores. On the way home, I stopped by the stables to visit for a few minutes with our friends there, humans and horses. After talking briefly with Carolyn, our friend and stable manager, I spent about ten minutes in the pasture with Red the horse. As I cried into her fur, I said some words like these to her, "I don't know what to say to you, sweet Red, but if you were human, I'd ask you to pray with us." Then I stroked her neck for a few moments, gave her some nibbles, and left.

Later that day, Carolyn told me that right after I left, she noticed that Red was down on the ground with her front legs folded up under her as if she were a foal, which is apparently not a common position for an adult horse. Red's nose was touching the ground, and her eyes were glazed over, as if she were in a trance. For a minute Carolyn was worried; then Red blinked her eyes and shook her head, and Carolyn realized she was okay. Who knows? I do know that Angela and Red had — and have — a special bond, and I believe that animals and other forms of life "know" more than we humans can begin to imagine. Angela, a Franciscan to her bones, believed this too.

In a few minutes, we will hear one of Angela's favorite choral pieces. "Adiemus," by English composer Karl Jenkins, is an example of "world music," in which there are no recognizable words from any language, but rather vocal sounds and rhythms that can cross cultures through the power of our imagination, so that whatever our cultures, the music may seem to reflect our voices and sounds. As much as any piece of music she knew, "Adiemus" represented to Angela what she hoped to convey about God through her sculptures and spiritual mentoring; through her work with horses and people with special needs who came to ride them; and through her life: that we are all in the Light — and that we share a vocation, all of us, to help create a world in which all of us can more fully realize that *this* is what it's all about!

How Angela would be loving this celebration and, of course, *is* loving every minute of it! After all, in the words of St. John Chrysostom, "She whom we love and lose is no longer where she was before. She is now wherever we are." "And that, daahlings, is the point." Amen.

Notes

1. "Turning/To the Women" for DLD, *Sacred Journeys: A Woman's Book of Daily Prayer* (Nashville: Upper Room Books, 1995), 187.

2. I speak here of "the United States" or "the United States of America" or "the U.S." rather than using the very popular term "America." The United States of America is, after all, one nation among many in the Americas. Many of our sisters and brothers from Canada to Chili are offended by what they experience as our arrogance in coopting the term "America" for ourselves alone. Since much of our history as a nation, especially in the latter part of the twentieth century, does point in this direction, I also am annoyed by our widespread, apparently oblivious, use of this term. To me, it has an imperious, arrogant ring, even though "America" is a lovely lyrical word that lends itself beautifully to hymns and songs!

3. I find myself, a white, professional-class Anglo descendant of a signer of the Declaration of Independence, wondering about sisters and brothers of other racial/ethnic groups in the U.S.: What is this terrorist climate like for them? Are our responses varying from group to group? Does this seem old and familiar to African and Native Americans who have long been subjected to our own brands of terrorism? What is it like, in the U.S. today, for Japanese, Korean, Vietnamese, and Cambodian Americans? For Haitians, Guatemalans, Filipinos, Chileans, Argentinians? For Jews from Eastern Europe and Jews from Israel who are living here now? For Palestinians in the United States, and Iraqis, Iranians, Afghanis? What is it like in the United States today for folks who are Irish, or who are Rwandans, Somalis, Bosnians, Croats, or Serbs? People around the world have experienced such atrocities in the names of God. Is this moment in the U.S., for many, a rerun of terrible times elsewhere or here in the United States for kids and adults for whom gangs, guns, drive-by shootings, and slaughter in schools have become constant sources of terror?

4. See Beverly Wildung Harrison, "The Power of Anger in the Work of Love," in *Making the Connections: Essays in Feminist Social Ethics*, ed. Carol S. Robb (Boston: Beacon, 1985).

5. This particular problem, as deeply spiritual and moral as economic and social, stands out in the context of the war on terrorism that the U.S. is currently waging against the Taliban (and, as things develop over time, probably others suspected of being or befriending terrorists). The Taliban (which

105

seems to be falling even as I write) has been notorious for its brutalizing of women. For this reason alone, many women throughout the world are probably joined through our ambivalence about the efforts of the U.S. and its allies to destroy the Taliban. On the one hand *if the victors include the women of Afghanistan* (a far from sure thing), the end of the Taliban could mean a new day dawning for girls and women in this desperately poor, war-torn Asian nation. On the other hand, the fact that the United States is dropping bombs on civilians, women and children included, means that we risk destroying the very people we intend to help. This is why increasing numbers of people in the United States and elsewhere have serious misgivings about how this war on terrorism is being waged. Even if the Taliban is successfully removed and a more democratic and woman-affirming regime comes to power, what will the United States do then? What if bin Laden is caught, or what if he isn't? Where beyond Afghanistan, and where beyond bin Laden, will we go with this war on terrorism?

6. See especially *Saving Jesus from Those Who Are Right: Rethinking What It Means to Be Christian* (Minneapolis: Fortress, 1999), and *The Redemption of God: A Theology of Mutual Relation* (Lanham, Md.: University Press of America, 1982).

7. I appreciate especially the insights of Eknath Easwaran (1978) on Gandhi.

8. The effort to make God imagery more inclusive of women's experiences has been moderately successful over the last couple of decades, especially in the United Church of Christ and the Unitarian Universalist Association and in ecumenical feminist movements and organizations, such as the Roman Catholic "Woman Church" movement and the "Re-Imagining" Conferences, which have been largely Protestant.

9. I will always be grateful to my theological mentor and good friend Tom F. Driver for helping me understand this. His book *Patterns of Grace: Human Experience as Word of God* (New York: Harper and Row, 1971) is an honest and brilliant examination of this foundational dimension of Christian theology.

10. This is why Elisabeth Schüssler Fiorenza prefers the term "kyriarchal" (meaning authoritarian domination) to "patriarchal." It's her way of trying to move beyond gender as the primary, much less sole, basis of oppression. She suggests, instead, that the issue is a complex one of domination in which gender, race, class, and other factors conspire to hold in place the power of privileged men. While I agree with Schüssler Fiorenza's desire to complexify the problem, I'm reluctant to let go of the problem of patriarchal power which is indeed *gendered*, albeit in complex ways. Too much Christian theology, like the Taliban version of Islam, is steeped in *patriarchal* violence. It is also racist, classist, anti-Semitic, and like most patriarchal religions far too anthropocentric (human-centered).

11. Carter Heyward, *Saving Jesus from Those Who Are Right: Rethinking What It Means to Be Christian* (Minneapolis: Fortress, 1999), 62.

12. See *Sisters in the Wilderness: The Challenge of Womanist God-Talk* (Maryknoll, N.Y.: Orbis, 1993).

13. See *The Redemption of God.*

14. I am buoyed by the classic example of St. Francis and the teachings of Albert Schweitzer. I'm also heartened by the current work of people of various spiritual traditions who share a commitment to helping create cultures of nonviolence toward animals and earth: Christian ethicists Larry Rasmussen, Dan Spencer, and Dieter Hessel; Christian feminist theologians Kwok Pui-lan and Sallie McFague; Queer theologian J. Michael Clark; religious philosophers Jay McDaniel and Christopher Key Chapple; feminist theologian Carol Adams; veterinarian Michael W. Fox; and writers and teachers such as Thomas Berry, Susan Chernak McElroy, and Joanna Macy.

Selected Readings

Althaus-Reid, Marcella. *Indecent Theology: Theological Perversions in Sex, Gender, and Politics.* London: Routledge, 2000.

Aronson, Elliot. *Nobody Left to Hate: Teaching Compassion after Columbine.* New York: Freeman, 2000.

Ashrawi, Hanan. *This Side of Peace.* New York: Touchstone, 1995.

Brock, Rita Nakashima, and Rebecca Ann Parker. *Proverb of Ashes: Violence, Redemptive Suffering, and the Search for What Saves Us.* Boston: Beacon, 2001.

Chapple, Christopher Key. *Nonviolence to Animals, Earth, and Self in Asian Traditions.* Albany: State University of New York Press, 1993.

Coward, Harold G. *Pluralism in the World Religions: A Short Introduction.* Oxford: Oneworld, 2000.

Douglas, Ian T., and Kwok Pui-lan, eds. *Beyond Colonial Anglicanism: The Anglican Communion in the Twenty-First Century.* New York: Church Publishing Inc., 2001.

Easwaran, Eknath. *Gandhi the Man.* Petaluma, Calif.: Nilgiri, 1978.

Enright, Robert D., and Joanna North, eds. *Exploring Forgiveness.* Madison: University of Wisconsin Press, 1998.

Esack, Farid. *Qur'an, Liberation, and Pluralism: An Islamic Perspective of Interreligious Solidarity against Oppression.* Oxford: Oneworld, 1997.

Gandhi, Mohandas K. *Autobiography: The Story of My Experiments with Truth.* New York: Dover, 1948, 1983.

Hanh, Thich Nhat. *Living Buddha, Living Christ.* New York: Riverhead, 1995.

———. *Love in Action: Writings on Nonviolent Social Change.* Berkeley, Calif.: Parallax, 1993.

Harrison, Beverly Wildung. *Making the Connections: Essays in Feminist Social Ethics.* Boston: Beacon, 1985.

Helmick, Raymond, S.J., and Rodney L. Petersen, eds. *Forgiveness and Reconciliation: Religion, Public Policy, and Conflict Transformation.* Radnor, Pa.: Templeton Foundation Press, 2001.

Heyward, Carter. *The Redemption of God: A Theology of Mutual Relation.* Lanham, Md.: University Press of America, 1982.

———. *Saving Jesus from Those Who Are Right: Rethinking What It Means to Be Christian.* Minneapolis: Fortress, 1999.

———. *Speaking of Christ: A Lesbian Feminist Voice.* Cleveland: Pilgrim, 1989.

Kwok Pui-lan. *Introducing Asian Feminist Theology.* Cleveland: Pilgrim, 2000.

Lerner, Michael. *Spirit Matters: Global Healing and the Wisdom of the Soul.* Charlottesville, Va.: Hampton Roads, 2000.

McCormick, Adele von Rüst, Ph.D., and Marlena Deborah McCormick, Ph.D. *Horse Sense and the Human Heart: What Horses Can Teach Us about Trust, Bonding, Creativity and Spirituality.* Deerfield Park, Fla., Health Communications, 1997.

McDaniel, Jay B. *Of God and Pelicans: A Theology for the Reverence of Life.* Louisville: Westminster/ John Knox, 1989.

Macy, Joanna. *Despair and Personal Power in the Nuclear Age.* Philadelphia: New Society, 1983.

Meyer, Marvin, and Charles Hughes, eds. *Jesus Then and Now: Images of Jesus in History and Christology.* Harrisburg, Pa.: Trinity, 2001.

Mollenkott, Virginia Ramey. *Omnigender: A Trans-Religious Approach.* Cleveland: Pilgrim, 2001.

Niebuhr, H. Richard. *Christ and Culture.* San Francisco: HarperSanFrancisco, 1951, 2001.

Nouwen, Henri J. M., Donald P. McNeill, and Douglas A. Morrison. *Compassion: A Reflection on the Christian Life.* New York: Doubleday, 1983.

Oduyoye, Mercy Amba. *Daughters of Anowa: African Women and Patriarchy.* Maryknoll, N.Y.: Orbis, 1995.

Rasmussen, Larry. *Earth Community, Earth Ethics.* Maryknoll, N.Y.: Orbis, 1996.

Richardson, Jan L. *Sacred Journeys: A Woman's Book of Daily Prayer.* Nashville: Upper Room Books, 1995.

Steinhoff Smith, Roy Herndon. *The Mutuality of Care.* St. Louis: Chalice, 1999.

Stepaniak, Joanne. *Being Vegan: Living with Conscience, Conviction, and Compassion.* Los Angeles: Lowell House, 2000.

Sturm, Douglas. *Solidarity and Suffering: Toward a Politics of Relationality.* Albany, N.Y.: SUNY, 1998.

Townes, Emilie M., ed. *Embracing the Spirit: Womanist Perspectives on Hope, Salvation, and Transformation.* Maryknoll, N.Y.: Orbis, 1997.

Tutu, Desmond. *No Future without Forgiveness.* New York: Image, 1999.

Washington, James M., ed. *A Testament of Hope: The Essential Writings of Martin Luther King, Jr.* San Francisco: Harper and Row, 1986.

Williams, Delores S. *Sisters in the Wilderness: The Challenge of Womanist God-Talk.* Maryknoll, N.Y.: Orbis, 1993.

Wink, Walter. *The Human Being: Jesus and the Enigma of the Son of Man.* Minneapolis: Fortress, 2001.

O Lord, support us all the day long, until the shadows lengthen, and the evening comes, and the busy world is hushed, and the fever of life is over, and our work is done. Then in thy mercy, grant us a safe lodging, and a holy rest, and peace at the last.

—From the Episcopal Book of Common Prayer